The TRINITY
REVEALED *in*
SCRIPTURE

AN OLD AND NEW TESTAMENT COMPARATIVE STUDY

MICHAEL D. BARRON

ISBN 979-8-88540-873-8 (paperback)
ISBN 979-8-88540-874-5 (digital)

Christian Faith Publishing
832 Park Avenue
Meadville, PA 16335
www.christianfaithpublishing.com

Printed in the United States of America

Soli Deo Gloria

To Rose Logan—Bogan, who took the precious time to tell me about having a personal relationship with Jesus Christ.

CONTENTS

PREFACE

❧

After reading this little book, my hope is that you will have a clear understanding of why Christians believe in the triune nature of God. God is a three-person being or "trinity." This is thoroughly taught in Scripture. From the Old Testament to the New Testament, the Bible reveals an almost inexhaustible pattern of scriptures relating to this fact: God is Father, Son, and Spirit. All you need to do is read and study the Bible. Look up the characteristics of God, His names, what is ascribed to Him—His traits, nature, attributes, qualities, and abilities. You will discover that our *one* God has three distinct personages.

Throughout Scripture, God shows Himself in remarkable ways. Whereas God has no corporeal (physical) form, for He is Spirit and Truth, He does appear as a theophany (a visible manifestation of God) in the Old Testament. In Genesis, it was He who wrestled Jacob all night; in 2 Samuel, it was He who marched on the tops of mulberry trees before David's men to conquer the Philistines; and in Daniel, it was He who was in the fire with the three young men as the "Son of God."

And in the New Testament, God the Son appears as a Christophany (a nonphysical manifestation of Jesus). In Acts it was Jesus who met Saul on the way to Damascus, and in the book of Mark, it was a theophany of the Spirit that appeared and descended like a dove upon Jesus, and it is only this Jesus that can open our hearts and minds to the truth (Luke 24:45). These appearances of our Lord should help us to understand Him. I believe these manifestations are there to aid in our ability to grasp His three-personage being.

In 1 Corinthians 14:33 (KJV) it says,

> For God is not *the author* of confusion, but of peace.

All of the Bible is consistent because God is consistent. You will find that from Genesis to Revelation, God does not change in His character. From the Bible, there were forty authors who wrote sixty-six books over a span of about 1,500 years. That's quite an accomplishment unless you are God, and then it's no big deal because HE can do anything. Look to see and understand the connections. To those that do not see the Trinity or refuse to believe it, I suggest you go before the Lord and ask Him to show Himself to you, to reveal His divine nature, and in humility, believe that HE will reveal Himself to you.

I have tried in these pages to convey the truth of God's Word in order to reveal His Trinity as it unfolds in Scripture—inshallah, "God willing," for my Muslim friends. As you read and examine the truth found in Scripture, I hope you allow God to speak to your heart. My prayer is that we would all believe in who HE is and that He is one—the one true God. As this is a study in book form, I encourage you to read just one chapter at a time, meditate on it, pray on it, and move on to the next chapter. By the time you are finished, you should have a pretty good grasp on why we Christians believe in God's triune nature.

I pray this book blesses all who read it and all who seek God.

Throughout this study, I will rely on the New King James Version (online), the King James Version, the English Standard Version (online), and the New Living Translation (online) of the Bible. They are accurate English translations. The King James Version of the Bible, though accurate, was written in the year 1611. I took the liberty of using some of the newer translations to provide the reader with a practical and contemporary interpretation. I would also like to mention that there are a few verses in Scripture that we will see more than once; this is due to the many verses in Scripture that share the same title, name of God, or character trait as my chapter subjects suggest. Remember, God's Word is good, and it is meant to be enjoyed. Read the Word enthusiastically and prayerfully, knowing He is revealing Himself to you. He loves you and wants to spend eternity with you.

INTRODUCTION

───────────── ❦ ─────────────

I had been a Christian for well over twenty-five years when my new friend Ahmad, a Muslim, asked me about the Trinity and if it is in the Bible. Though I felt very comfortable in my beliefs, having studied Christianity for several years, I paused at this opportunity to give much of a reply. I mentioned the Old Testament passage in Isaiah 9:6 (KJV), which speaks about the coming Messiah:

> For unto us a child is born, unto us a son is given; and the government will be upon his shoulder: and his name will be called Wonderful, Counselor, mighty God, The everlasting Father, The Prince of Peace.

I also told Ahmad about the Gospel of John in the New Testament. John 1:1 (KJV) says the same thing about Jesus:

> In the beginning was the Word, and the Word was with God, and the Word was God.

Then in John 1:14 (KJV), it says,

> And the Word was made flesh, and dwelt among us.

Thinking he'd be satisfied with that, he asked, "Did Jesus ever say that He was God?"

Oh boy, I hesitated. In keeping the dialogue honest, I had to tell him that no, Jesus never directly said the phrase "I am God." Collecting my thoughts, I told Ahmad that Jesus does say that He is, indeed, God. He qualifies Himself as God and defines Himself as God and shares the same attributes associated with God. As a matter of fact, while comforting His disciples, Jesus says about the Father in John 14:7 (NKJV):

> If you had known Me, you would have known My Father also; and from now on you know Him and have seen Him.

This is a bold statement for sure. Jesus has just referred to Himself as God. We know this because in the very next verse, His disciple Philip says in John 14:8 (KJV),

> Lord, shew us the Father, and it sufficeth us.

And Jesus replies in John 14:9 (KJV),

> Have I been so long time with you, and yet hast thou not known me, Philip? He that hath seen me hath seen the Father; and how sayest thou *then*, shew us the Father?

Case closed! Jesus just said that He is God again. Still, my friend didn't seem to get it, so I tried a different approach. I had thought about giving him the apple example. You may know the illustration where an apple is presented as having three parts: the skin, the fruit, and the core. Even though the apple is three parts, it is still just one apple. Or how about the egg example in which you have the shell, the albumen (white), and the yolk? Again three parts, yet only one egg.

Either example presents a pretty good illustration about how something could be three in one. However, ultimately any example I could use seems almost sinful when trying to explain the triune nature of an all-powerful, all-knowing God, so I gave Ahmad the best idea that came to mind in the moment. I told him that I was just one guy. He agreed. I'm a father, a son, and a husband. I have three basic personages. Even though I have three personages, I am still just one guy. I can do something as a father, I can do something as a husband, and I can do something else as a son—totally independent of my other roles. This is a trinity of sorts. Looking back, a better example may have been to say that I have a *physical body* (representing the Son), a *conscious mind* (representing the Father), and a *spirit/soul* (representing the Holy Spirit).

God, in His divine nature, is a Trinity as well. He is the Father, He is the Son, and He is the Spirit—the Holy Spirit. This is clearly taught in Scripture. In the first book of the Bible, Genesis, it mentions the plurality of God. In Genesis 1:26a (NLT), we read,

> Then God said, "Let Us make human beings in our image, to be like us."

Who was God talking to? Angels perhaps? No, certainly not! God did not need any angelic help in making man—He made the angels too.

Remember, in the first verse of Genesis (KJV), it says,

> In the beginning God created the heaven and the earth.

And in Isaiah 43:7 (NKJV), it says,

> Everyone who is called by My Name, whom I have created for My glory; I have formed him, yes, I have made him.

So when God created everything, He was speaking in His own triune personage as Father, Son, and Spirit. When He said, "Let *us* make human beings," *Elohim* is the word used for *God* in Hebrew, and it is grammatically a plural noun—one God with three distinct centers of consciousness.

After we had parted ways, there was still this lingering uneasiness that stayed with me. I didn't feel as though I had done my job well. I kept telling myself that it wasn't up to me but the Holy Spirit to convict someone of the truth about God. I prayed a lot as I drove home. It became clear to me that I would have to do some serious studying if I wanted a different outcome next time, so I began a study of the Trinity. I looked up verses that supported the doctrine of the Trinity and of the names of God and of His attributes. Verse by verse, the Trinity of God became ever more apparent.

The names of God are explicit and His character sure. His wisdom, power, and love are endless! In fact, the names of God kept pointing clearly to God the Father and God the Son. *Wow! This is radical*, I thought.

When you look up one of God's names, you end up learning another. Interestingly, that second name identifies with the first. I looked up both *Maker* and *Creator*, which are words that we associate with God. What I found was remarkable! *Maker* in the Old Testament was synonymous with *Creator*, LORD, and *the Holy One of Israel*. I did not know *Maker*, LORD, and *the Holy One of Israel* were used interchangeably. As an example, in Isaiah 45:11 (KJV), God says,

> Thus saith the LORD, the Holy One of Israel, and his Maker.

I took this verse and compared the use of the title "Holy One" as it appears in the New Testament with Acts 3:14 (KJV), which says of the Lord,

> But ye denied the Holy One and the Just, and desired a murderer to be granted unto you.

This is a specific reference to Jesus. Acts 3:14 reminds us that the Jews chose to let Barabbas, a murderer, go free and Jesus, the Holy One, to be condemned (Matthew 27:17–26).

It was about this time that I felt the Lord telling me to do something about it. Well, I'm not a professional writer. I thought a book was out. I'm not a pastor and felt a sermon was out as well. Thinking to myself, *Okay, God if you're going to put something on my heart that might help the young in faith or the spiritually challenged to see and understand the Trinity, then You are going to have to help me.* With His inspiration, the least I could do was to sit down and give it my best shot. With this task in mind, my study began.

What I decided to do was to start in the Old Testament with the names, titles, and attributes of God then move on to find them in the New Testament, a biblical comparative of sorts. For instance, the word *King* in the Old Testament refers to God. When we read of the [K]ing in the New Testament, it refers to Jesus Christ. It would appear that both God the Father and Jesus the Son are Kings. Are they two separate Kings or one? Though not obvious, by reading Revelation 19:16 (NKJV), we can understand that the *two* are indeed one. As we read of Jesus glorified,

> And He has on *His* robe and on His thigh
> a name written: KING OF KINGS AND LORD OF
> LORDS.

If God is *King* and we read that Jesus is *King of kings*, then They must be one of the same, for no one could be higher than God. There are literally hundreds and hundreds of corresponding verses throughout Scripture that show these types of parallels.

One simple scripture in the New Testament that shows evidence for there being a Trinity would be in Luke 3:22 (KJV) when Jesus had just been baptized:

> And the Holy Ghost descended in a bodily
> shape like a dove upon him, and a voice came

from heaven, which said, "Thou art my beloved
Son; in thee I am well pleased."

I think this is a fairly obvious declaration about God's triune
nature. However, there are many more than this. The Bible is jam-
packed with passages concerning the doctrine of the Trinity. From
"Savior" to the "One Who heals" to "the One Who is called the First
and the Last," it's all there for us in the Word of God. As you read
these chapters, ask the Lord for wisdom and discernment, understanding, and a heart for the truth. As 1 Thessalonians 5:21 (KJV)
says,

Prove all things; hold fast that which is
good.

CHAPTER 1

⌘

SAVIOR

If you ask a Christian who the *Savior* is, you are likely to hear something like "Jesus, of course." I would have to agree. My favorite example of the trinity is the triune God as Savior. In the New Testament, Jesus is mentioned as Savior several times. Nonetheless, the first time we read of a Savior is not in the New Testament but in the Old Testament. In 2 Samuel 22:3 (NKJV) (probably written sometime between 630–540 BC) we read,

> The God of my strength, in whom I will
> trust; My shield and the horn of my salvation,
> My stronghold and my refuge; My Savior, You
> save me from violence.

In this song of deliverance, David is declaring God to be his Savior. I purposely showed the entire verse so that you would understand in context whom David is alluding to as the Savior. Most of the time, it will not be necessary to show the entire verse, so I won't. Even in the Psalms, God is again referred to as the Savior. Psalm 106:21 (NLT) says,

> They forgot God, their savior, who had
> done such great things in Egypt.

The Bible is clear and consistent. As we continue to read a few more verses, you will notice that wherever there is a Savior mentioned, there will most likely be an attribute, a name, title, or characteristic attached to it. In Isaiah 43:11 (KJV), it says,

> I *even* I, *am* the LORD; and beside Me *there*
> *is* no saviour.

I don't know if God can make it any simpler than that. He just said that He is LORD and that there is no other Savior other than Himself.

We see this again in Isaiah 60:16 (NKJV):

> You shall drink the milk of the Gentiles,
> and milk the breast of kings; You shall know that
> I, the LORD, *am* your Savior and your Redeemer,
> the Mighty One of Jacob.

I love this about God. He says things over and over so that we can wrap our minds around something and get it. So what do we know so far about Who the Savior is from the Old Testament? We know that

- God was David's Savior.
- The LORD is Savior, and there is no other.
- The Redeemer is Savior.
- The Mighty One of Jacob is Savior.

So that there is no mistaking just who the Savior is, let's just look at one more verse, and then we'll compare these scriptures to those found in the New Testament. Isaiah 45:21 (KJV) states,

> *Who* hath told it from that time? *Have* not
> I the LORD? And *there is* no God else beside me;
> a just God and a Savior; *there is* none beside me.

This should bring us much comfort. God is not some aloof or distant god who vacillates or is indecisive, mystical, and out of reach. He is personable and purposeful, telling us plainly who He is. He wants us to know Him. People were worshiping many gods at this time (and still do today). God, in His Word, says over and over that He is our only God and only Savior.

Let's take a look at what the New Testament has to say about the Savior. The first mention of Savior is found in the Gospel of Luke. It is no coincidence that the first time we read the title of *Savior* in the New Testament, it is directed at God the Father and not Jesus the Son. This is because Jesus had not yet been born, and the gospels (the first four books of the New Testament: Matthew, Mark, Luke, and John) had not been written yet. Though the gospels are the inspired Word of God which chronicle the life of Jesus, it is important to understand that the church age and spread of Christianity hadn't taken place yet. Jesus was first referred to as Savior in the Acts of the apostles, which is the book immediately following the gospels.

In the Gospel of Luke, Mary is visited by the angel Gabriel *"who stands in the presence of God"* (Luke 1:19 NKJV). He tells Mary the most shocking and wonderful thing she could ever hear. Mary is told by the angel in Luke 1:28–33 that she has found favor with God and she will have a Son, He will inherit the throne of David, and His kingdom will have no end. Hallelujah! Could you imagine the angel Gabriel coming to any one of us and saying that we have God's favor and that our son would be the fulfillment of His promise of a Savior? This grand promise was the arrival of the eternal King. I could only imagine what she must have thought.

Mary then visits her relative Elizabeth, who is pregnant in her *"old age"* with the one who would be called John the Baptist. When Mary steps into the room, the unborn baby in Elizabeth's womb is filled with the Holy Spirit (Luke 1:41). Elizabeth says the next coolest thing ever in verse 43 (NKJV) where she asks of Mary,

> But why is this granted to me, that the mother of my Lord should come to me?

I love that! Elizabeth, being filled with the Holy Spirit, knew who was in Mary's womb—the Lord!

You may think this is a little side story, but I have included it so that you would understand why Mary says what she does in Luke 1:47 (ESV), where she proclaims,

> And my spirit rejoices in God my Savior.

What a beautiful statement by Mary, confessing God as her Savior as she knows without a doubt that she will be giving birth to the Messiah Jesus. Luke 2:11 (NKJV) says,

> For there is born to you this day in the city
> of David a Savior, who is Christ the Lord.

If you are a new believer or not a believer at all, this may have you scratching your head. In the first chapter of Luke, we read that God is our Savior, and then we're told that Christ is our Savior. Are there two Saviors? *Istaghfurallah* ("God forbid" in Arabic for my Muslim friends)! We have already learned in the Old Testament that there is only one God and one Savior though now the dynamic of who the Savior is has changed. Indeed, when the Son was born, the promised Messiah, the prophecy of Isaiah 9:6 (NKJV), came true!

> For unto us a Child is born, unto us a
> Son is given; And the government will be upon
> His shoulder. And His name will be called
> Wonderful, Counselor, Mighty God, Everlasting
> Father, Prince of Peace.

Next, let's take a look at what others say about Jesus Christ. In John 4:39 (NKJV), the Samaritan woman said about Jesus, "He told me all that I ever did." Following in verse 42, it says,

> Then they said to the woman, "Now we
> believe, not because of what you said, for we our-

selves have heard *Him* and we know that this is
indeed the Christ, the Savior of the world."

This is amazing stuff, guys! Whether they knew it or not,
the Samaritans were calling Jesus God by giving Him the title of
Savior. In Acts 5:31 (NKJV), we're told by Peter and others that God
appoints Jesus as Savior, where we read,

> Him God has exalted to His right hand *to
> be* Prince and Savior, to give repentance to Israel
> and forgiveness of sins.

So in the Old Testament, God declares Himself as Savior, and
now He elevates Jesus to that same status in the New Testament. One
should reason then that both are God because God does not lie. He
is always true and consistent. This may be hard to understand. How
could both God and Jesus be Savior at the same time? Simple—Jesus
is God the Son.

Remember in the introduction where I said I was a father, a
son, and a husband but still just one guy? God is three personages
also. He is Father, Son, and Spirit. We'll explore Who the Spirit is in
a little while (though I think I just gave it away). Jesus Christ has a
uniqueness about Him that is different than any other human being
who has ever lived. No person has ever said legitimately as Jesus did
when He said in John 17:5 (KJV),

> And now, O Father, glorify thou me with
> thine own self with the glory which I had with
> thee before the world was.

What was that? Jesus is talking about the relationship that He
had with the Father before the world was created, and let's remember this about God's glory—God says in Isaiah 42:8 that He does
not share His glory with anyone. Therefore, we must conclude that
They are uniquely one. In Genesis, God said, "*Let us make man in
Our image.*" Jesus, the Spirit, and the Father shared a glorious eternal

majesty together before creation and time, and this inference of pre-scribing deity to Christ and the Holy Spirit is throughout the Bible.

Before we finish up with the Savior, I'd like to share just one more verse of Christ's uniqueness. I think it will help us to under-stand how both God the Father and Jesus Christ are both Savior and God. Philippians 2:6 (KJV) says about Jesus,

> Who, being in the form of God, thought it
> not robbery to be equal with God.

Heresy, right? Well, it would be if it were applied to any other man. However, it was not; it solely applies to our Savior Jesus Christ. Seriously, could you imagine anyone thinking it was reasonable or somehow all right to consider themselves equal with God, the Creator of the universe? This is where some Mormons, Muslims and Jehovah's Witnesses get it wrong. Jesus is not merely a god. Jesus is not just a sinless prophet or a man who became the god of this world. Jesus is God!

If you are starting to get this, thank the Holy Spirit. It is His job to put Christ and God the Father together, for it says throughout Scripture that the Spirit of God gives wisdom and understanding. Exodus 31:3 (KJV) expresses it this way:

> And I have filled him with the spirit of God,
> in wisdom, and in understanding, and in knowl-
> edge, and in all manner of workmanship.

We can wrap up who the Savior is with just a couple more verses. Paul, in his letter to Titus in chapter 2 verse 13 (NKJV), says this about Christ:

> Looking for the blessed hope and glorious
> appearing of our great God and Savior Jesus
> Christ.

This is so cool. Paul is who I'd call the "top dog" of the apostles, and he just said that Jesus is both God and Savior. You should know that Paul wasn't your average guy. Paul was a Pharisee, well known as an intellectual, cultured, and a scholar.

We'll read just one more verse on the Savior. The disciple Simon Peter, who wrote 2 Peter, says in chapter 1 verse 1 (NLT) about Jesus,

> I am writing to you who share the same pre-
> cious faith we have. This faith was given to you
> because of the justice and fairness of Jesus Christ,
> our God and Savior.

There you have it—Jesus's own disciples called Him both God and Savior. No one should doubt that between the Old and New Testament, the overwhelming evidence points to both God and Jesus Christ as being our Savior. Let's also remember that there is only One God, and he is true and consistent.

What we now know:

- There is only one Savior.
- God is Savior.
- Jesus is Savior.

CHAPTER 2

ᏇᏏ

WHO RAISED JESUS FROM THE DEAD?

Before we discuss who raised Jesus from the dead, let's first look at who killed Jesus. You may have been told that Jesus was killed by the Jews or that the Roman guards did it. You may have even heard people say that you or I, by our sin, killed Him. Any of the three would make sense but are wrong. It may surprise you to know that none of us killed Him. In keeping things straightforward, as has been my mission, the one who killed Jesus was *Jesus*! That's right. Now let me clarify. Jesus did not actually take His own life. After all, we know that He was brutally beaten and nailed to a cross. What I'm saying here is that He had complete control over His own life and death. Jesus makes this abundantly clear when He speaks of His life this way in John 10:18 (ESV):

> No one takes it from Me, but I lay it down
> of my own accord. I have authority to lay it

down, and I have authority to take it up again.
This charge I have received from My Father.

Even in the verse before, in John 10:17 (NKJV), we read Jesus saying,

Therefore My Father loves Me, because I lay
down My life that I may take it again.

Clearly Jesus said that no one took His life. He laid it down willingly for you and me. You could say that it was *His love for us* that killed Him.

His death was prophesied long before He was even born in Isaiah 53 and in Psalm 22. In fact, there are probably well over one hundred prophecies concerning His life and death.

With regard to Jesus's power over life and death, we should consider His relationship to life. In Acts 3:15 (KJV), it talks about Jesus being murdered. The passage says,

And killed the Prince of life, whom God
hath raised from the dead, whereof we are
witnesses.

Pretend you don't know Who raised Jesus from the dead for now. Do look at that use of the title "'Prince of life" referring to Jesus in Acts 3:15. This is another great title of our Lord. In the New Living Translation, it calls Jesus the "Author of life." I think both are appropriate for Jesus's nature. Only God, His Spirit, or the Son of God could hold such a title as this. Indeed, Jesus has an inherent quality that places Him above all others. John 6:40 (NKJV) sums it up this way:

And this is the will of Him who sent Me,
that everyone who sees the Son and believes in
Him may have everlasting life; and I will raise
him up at the last day.

By this verse, it is evident that our hope of having eternal life comes by faith in Jesus Christ. Indeed, we have a God and Savior who loves us so much that He gave His Son as payment for our sin. All we have to do is believe. A little later in the Gospel of John, Jesus's identity with life is revealed this way. John 11:25 (NLT) quotes Jesus:

> I am the resurrection and the life. Anyone
> who believes in me will live, even after dying.

His great promise of eternal life! Further, in John 14:6 (NLT), Jesus clarifies,

> I am the way, the truth, and the life. No one
> can come to the Father except through Me.

Well, there you have it. Jesus says that He is life and that He is the only way to God the Father. That statement is not ambiguous in any way.

Now we know that Jesus is life and that no one can take His life. The question still remains: "Who raised Jesus from the dead?" Well, we have just read a few moments ago in Acts 3:15 that God raised Jesus. Did anyone else raise Him back to life besides God? Let us see. We are told in Scripture that Jesus was not only raised by God the Father but by Jesus Christ Himself and the Holy Spirit. It is an excellent example of the Trinity at work; and even though God only needs to say something once, the Bible repeats that God raised Jesus. In Acts 2:32 (ESV), Luke confirms,

> This Jesus God raised up, and of that we are
> all witnesses.

Also in Acts 5:30 (ESV):

> The God of our fathers raised Jesus, whom
> you killed by hanging him on a tree.

You probably noticed that it says "whom you murdered" in this verse and are thinking, *Wait a minute. You said that none of us killed Him, and here it says "murdered."* Remember that Jesus laid down his life willingly and was murdered.

And lastly, in Acts 10:40 (NKJV):

> Him God raised up on the third day, and showed Him openly.

There are several more verses, but let's go back to what Jesus said. Remember when we read John 10:17–18, where Jesus said that He could lay His life down and take it up again? That's not all He said. He addressed His life and His power over death again in John 2:19 (NKJV) while turning over tables and using a whip to drive out the moneychangers in the temple. The Jews questioned His authority to do this, and Jesus answered them by saying,

> Destroy this temple, and in three days I will raise it up.

The Jews didn't get it; He was speaking of raising Himself up back to life. Nevertheless, the apostle John explains to us what Jesus meant in John 2:21 (NLT):

> But when Jesus said "this temple," he meant his own body.

Here again—Jesus raising Himself from the dead, his unique authority over life being displayed. This is the same authority that God unveils in His written Word about Himself. Both the Father and the Son share this unmistakable sovereign power.

We have a great gift in Christ Jesus and in the ransom He paid for us. Jesus not only offers us life but eternal life, as Romans 6:23 (NKJV) says:

> For the wages of sin *is* death, but the gift of
> God *is* eternal life in Christ Jesus our Lord.

God's gift to us is eternal life in His Son Jesus Christ, and let's not forget what we've learned in John 14:6, when Jesus said that He is the way, the truth, and the life. Well, I think we're getting it.

So, how about the Spirit? The third personage of the Holy Trinity is a little less understood than God the Father or God the Son. God the Holy Spirit appears to be somewhat mystical, ethereal, or abstract in nature. That is because it is God the Holy Spirit's job to put both God the Father and Jesus Christ the Son together and *to make Them known*. It is not for Him to bring glory to Himself but to direct glory and honor to God through Jesus Christ. In keeping this a biblical comparative, I'd like to look at the Holy Spirit's own power with and over life. As Jesus enters time and the world, we read that the Spirit has been the one to cause Mary, mother of Jesus, to be with child. Matthew 1:18 (NKJV) says,

> She was found with child of the Holy Spirit.

I believe that there are some things this side of heaven that we will just not fully understand. I'm not sure how great or all-powerful God would be if I could understand Him completely anyway. With that in mind, two verses later in Matthew 1:20 (ESV), an angel (messenger) of the Lord says to Mary's husband-to-be Joseph,

> Joseph, son of David, do not fear to take
> Mary as your wife, for that which is conceived in
> her is from the Holy Spirit.

This may or may not give you much help. Mary conceived Jesus by the Spirit of God. Maybe this will ease our understanding, knowing that God is working through the Holy Spirit. Definitely, the Trinity is at work here. All three—the Father, the Son, and the Holy Spirit—have an expressed rule or charge over life from the womb to beyond the tomb. It is interesting that when Jesus died on the cross, the Bible says in Matthew 27:50 (ESV),

> And Jesus cried out again with a loud voice
> and yielded up his Spirit.

This is a bold declaration for sure. Jesus died when He yielded up His Spirit. This is because the Bible says in John 6:63 (NKJV),

> It is the Spirit who gives life.

Whoa, the Spirit is the One Who gives life? Absolutely! It is abundantly clear the Spirit's power over life is just like that of the Father and the Son. Romans (one of my favorite books of the Bible) says in chapter 8, verse 11 (KJV) who also raised Jesus:

> But if the Spirit of him that raised up Jesus
> from the dead dwell in you, he that raised up
> Christ from the dead shall also quicken your
> mortal bodies by his Spirit that dwelleth in you.

It doesn't get much more transparent than that. We have now read that Jesus was raised from the dead by the Spirit, God the Father, and Jesus Himself. All three are one. Can we express one final notion? Though we have read that Jesus is life and that it is the Spirit Who gives life, I'd like to add that it is also God the Father Who shares this uniqueness. As it says in 1 Timothy 6:13 (NKJV),

> I urge you in the sight of God who gives life
> to all things.

We can be sure that it is the Father, the Son, and the Spirit who orchestrate and have complete jurisdiction over life.

What we know now:

- God raised Jesus.
- Jesus raised Himself.
- His Spirit raised Jesus.

CHAPTER 3

❧

THE HOLY SPIRIT IS GOD

Is the Spirit of God truly God Himself? I'd dare say that most Christians would not want to answer this question—not because He is not, for He most certainly is, but because they wouldn't know how to give an answer. If you are not thoroughly educated in Scripture, it can be a tough nut to crack. Throughout both the Old and New Testament, *the Spirit* or *Holy Spirit* is mentioned some 523 times. I encourage you to get, if you have not already, a good Bible app. Research the word *Spirit*. It will astonish you as to what is attributed to the Spirit. We first read of the Spirit in the second verse of Genesis in the Old Testament. I find it fascinating that right at the beginning of creation, there is the Spirit, actively involved. In Genesis 1:2 (KJV) we read,

> And the Spirit of God moved upon the face
> of the waters.

So before God created man, there was the Spirit. He was with God during creation and there in Genesis 1:26 (KJV) when God said,

> Let us make man in our image, after our
> likeness:

It may surprise you to know that much is said about the Spirit in Scripture. As I have mentioned earlier, as you read these Bible verses, ask the Lord to give you wisdom and understanding. This will cultivate your faith, strengthen your walk, and ultimately, bring glory to God.

The Spirit seems to have a long list of duties, responsibilities, and traits associated with Him. Of course, being God the Spirit, it's infinite. By reading a few of the Holy Spirit's roles, we can get a better understanding as to His triune nature and purpose. We have already learned that the Spirit gives life and that it was by Him that Jesus was raised from the dead. We also read in Exodus 31:3 that the Spirit of God gives us wisdom, understanding, and knowledge.

What else does the Bible have to say about the Spirit? I think you will be impressed to know that Jesus says in John 4:24 (KJV),

> God *is* a Spirit: and they worship him must
> worship *him* in spirit and in truth.

Awesome, right? God is Spirit—and that's not all. Additionally Paul refers to Jesus as the Lord, and in 2 Corinthians 3:17 (NKJV), he says,

> Now the Lord is the Spirit; and where the
> Spirit of the Lord *is*, there *is* liberty.

This just keeps getting better. We have just read that both God and the Lord (Jesus) are the Spirit.

Remember what I said earlier about one word, title, or attribute identifying with the one before it? It just happened again. The

Lord's Word is fascinating for sure. He has just shown us His triune nature again. When I read verses like these, I am reminded of why Jesus said what He did in John 5:39 (ESV) concerning searching the Scriptures:

> You search the Scriptures because you think
> that in them you have eternal life; and it is they
> that bear witness about me.

Absolutely, Lord! Remember, the New Testament had not yet been written when Jesus referred to "the Scriptures." Jesus's reference was to the Old Testament when He said this. Fascinating.

Time for a quick review.

We know that God is Spirit, the Lord is the Spirit, and there is only one God. This is actually a lot to take in. Wrapping your head around God being a Spirit or three-in-one being isn't easy. However, as we look at more and more Scripture, our understanding of the Holy Spirit and of His triune nature that is shared between the Father and the Son will become more clear. Let's look at Matthew 28:19:

> Go therefore and make disciples of all the
> nations, baptizing them in the Name of the
> Father and of the Son and of the Holy Spirit.

Unmistakably a clear allusion to the Trinity! After all, why would we be told to go out and baptize people in the name of the Father, the Son, and the Holy Spirit if there were no Trinity and if They were not equal? Wouldn't it simply be enough to baptize folks in the name of the Father alone? What could the Son or Spirit add if God the Father was only God? Now, we aren't 100 percent sure if Jesus ever said this exactly; there is discrepancy in the Word as to when this was added. However, it unmistakably points to God's triune nature between His three-personage being.

Furthermore, there are other verses that direct us to God and His Spirit. In Galatians 4:5, to redeem those who were under the law, it says in chapter 4 verse 6 (NKJV),

> And because you are sons, God has sent forth the Spirit of His Son into your hearts, crying out, "Abba, Father!"

This is definitely great news. God (Father) sends us the (Holy) Spirit of His Son (Jesus) into our hearts. I hope the parentheses help. You will notice the union that is shared in that scripture. When we accept Christ, it is an amazing thing to comprehend that God adopted us as His children and put the Holy Spirit in our hearts so that we could call God "Daddy"—which is the meaning of "Abba."

Let's look at another approach to the Spirit as God. In the three synoptic gospels (meaning many of the same stories/perspective) that are in the New Testament, Matthew, Mark, and Luke all make mention of a man calling Jesus "Good Teacher." Jesus responds this way in Mark 10:18 (ESV):

> Why do you call me good? No one is good except God alone.

Now we know that Jesus is good, so why the rebuke? Did the man not realize or consider who Jesus was? Was Jesus saying that He wasn't good and, therefore, not God? Of course not! Jesus was sinless and perfect. What He was saying was (Mike's translation), "If you are referring to Me as the one and only God, then I am good and I am God. You are right in saying that as only God is good."

We can gain understanding of this when we consider what the Bible says about the Spirit as we read Psalm 143:10 (NKJV):

> For You *are* my God; Your Spirit is good.

So Jesus said that only God is good, and now we have just read that the Spirit is good. Does it seem as though the Bible is giving conflicting statements? Well, not exactly. Cult groups like to point out verses like Mark 10:18 to show that the Bible is not trustworthy. However, that is because they refuse to believe in the triune nature of God. They refuse to believe that Jesus is God in the flesh. It is because of their unbelief, not because of the written word, so they attack the Bible, God's written word. When they point to this verse and say that Jesus Himself said that He was not good, I like to remind them that He does say that He is, indeed, good. Matter of fact, He says it twice—once in John 10:11 and the other in John 10:14. In both verses, the meaning is the same, so we'll read just one. In John 10:11 (KJV), Jesus says,

> I am the good shepherd: the good shepherd
> giveth his life for the sheep.

Once more, the trinity of God is revealed with this description. Jesus said that only God is good and here; He just said that He was good. It's kind of funny, sitting here, looking at my notes on the Spirit, and thinking, *God, Your Spirit seems so limitless.* Duh! He is limitless because He is God.

There are literally hundreds of verses that relate equally between the Father, the Spirit, and the Son. God's omnifarious being is inexhaustible, too big and too overwhelming to describe completely. I could show twenty to thirty more verses that would identify His nature. However, I feel that it might read a little tedious and cause confusion. That said, we'll look at only a couple more verses that are pertinent to the Spirit's triune essence. First, Psalm 139:7 (NKJV) states,

> Where can I go from Your Spirit? Or where
> can I flee from Your presence?

This is an obvious rhetorical question. The psalmist knows that there is literally nowhere he can go to escape God's Spirit as God is infinite. Then in Micah 2:7 (NKJV), we read almost the same thing as it says,

> Is the Spirit of the LORD restricted?

No, He certainly is not. The Spirit is omnipresent (everywhere), omnipotent (all-powerful), and omniscient (all-knowing). This nature is only present in HIS being. Still, there are more passages about the Spirit that reflect this point. If you're thinking, *Okay, I get that God and the Spirit are everywhere at once, but what about Jesus?* We know that Jesus was not physically everywhere at once while he was on earth. After all, He was 100 percent man. However, He shares the same attributes ascribed to God the Father and God the Holy Spirit. Not wanting to spoil the next few chapters, I'd rather not comment too much on Jesus just yet. I will say for now that the magnitude of Christ, His Majesty, is powerful, flawless, and endless!

Lastly, concerning the Spirit, I'd like us to go to the book of Acts. In Acts chapter 5, we read of a husband and wife named Ananias and Sapphira. The couple and the other believers in their town were selling their personal goods and giving their proceeds to the followers of Jesus by laying them at the apostles' feet. This was supposed to be shared as a tithe to the Lord. Ananias and his wife kept part of their proceeds back and lied to everyone, including the apostles, to get them to believe that they gave all the income from the sale of their possession. The couple was not required to give anything, but by lying and trying to deceive those around them, we find out who they actually lied to when Peter challenged Ananias's deception in Acts 5:3 (NLT):

> Ananias, why have you let Satan fill your
> heart? You lied to the Holy Spirit, and kept some
> of the money for yourself.

Plainly, the apostle Peter told Ananias that he lied to the Holy Spirit. Peter then basically says, "Look, Ananias, the land was yours, and you could do whatever you wanted with it. Why did you misrepresent what you gave?" Here's the catch. Peter says in Acts 5:4 (NLT),

You weren't lying to us but to God!

Shocking, huh? The apostle Peter first says that Ananias lied to the Holy Spirit, and now, Peter clarifies that he lied to God. I think the reasonable conclusion we can draw from this is that God and the Holy Spirit are one.

What we now know:

- God is good.
- The Spirit is good.
- Jesus is good.
- The Spirit is God.
- The Lord is Spirit.
- Jesus is Lord.
- A lie to the Spirit is a lie to God.

CHAPTER 4

WHO HEALS?

Though there are some words or verses in Scripture that may seem vague, obscure, or ill-defined, the vast majority of them are not. Some words or phrases will even have more than one meaning. For example, in reading the New Testament, the word *love* has four primary meanings in the original Greek. They are

- *Phileo*—to like, or having brotherly love
- *Agape*—which is unconditional love
- *Storge*—the natural love for your child, family, or spouse
- *Eros*—the romantic or erotic love

The Greek actually has more words for *love*; however, I don't believe they are used in Scripture. These four Greek forms of love mentioned in Scripture describe a particular type or meaning of love. In English, we just use the one word—*love*. Words such as this have caused disparity between believers and churches alike. Many debates have occurred over the years as theologians have tried to define the true meaning of verses or phrases in Scripture. It is always important, therefore, to read the Bible in its proper context.

This is another reason why I wanted to give Scripture examples from the Old Testament first and then from the New. The Old Testament, which was first written in Hebrew, is not only a historical account of God's people but also the written law of the Jews and is a detailed account of where we first meet God. What we read about God, His nature, His identity, and His authority are all revealed in the Old Testament. For the New Testament to be true, it would need to harmonize or correlate with the Old Testament. With this in mind, I'd like to share who the Old Testament says is the One who heals. In Deuteronomy 32:39 (KJV), we read,

> See now that I, *even* I, am he, and there is no God with Me: I kill, and I make alive; I wound and I heal.

Well, that's pretty straightforward. God says that there is no God besides Him and that it is He who heals. This message is taught throughout the Bible. As an example, in 2 Kings 5:7 (KJV), we read about the king of Israel responding to a man sent to him for healing of leprosy:

> *Am* I God, to kill and make alive, that this man doth send unto me to recover a man of his of leprosy?

Despite being an evil king, King Jehoram applies Scripture here. The continuity of the Word does not change. This is surely an example for us to follow, for His Word is the sword of the Spirit and consistent throughout.

As is the norm, there are several more verses that mention God healing or being asked to heal in the Old Testament. Consequently, I need to show only a couple more for us to get a good understanding.

In Numbers 12, we read about Moses leading the people in the wilderness. Miriam (his sister) and Aaron (his brother) bring an accusation against Moses, questioning his authority. What Miriam and Aaron did angered the LORD, speaking out against Moses in their pride. This caused the LORD to leave their presence. When the LORD left, the cloud of God's manifestation (Shekinah glory) also departed. Miriam's skin was instantly as white as snow for she had become a leper. Aaron immediately repented and apologized to God, and in Numbers 12:13 (NLT), Moses prays:

> So Moses cried out to the LORD, "O God, I
> beg you, please heal her!"

This is a big deal that Moses immediately cries out to the LORD. For one, he knew Who was in control and Who was the only one with the power to heal. The other thing that it tells us is that Moses was faithful, as God said, and an example for us to follow. Miriam was cast outside the camp for seven days but upon being healed was allowed back in.

Another example of God as healer is when the psalmist in Psalm 30:2 (KJV) extols,

> O LORD my God, I cried unto thee, and
> thou hast healed me.

This is a psalm that occurred on or about the time of the dedication of David's temple and is meant as a song of thanksgiving. Read the entire psalm if you want the full context. You will find that the psalmist was expressing praise to God as he cried out in thanks for God's deliverance. It is an illustration of how the LORD's power can work in us for healing.

Isaiah 61:1 (NKJV) says,

> The Spirit of the Lord GOD *is* upon Me,
> Because the LORD has anointed Me To preach
> good tidings to the poor; He has sent Me to heal
> the brokenhearted.

This is really cool. On our own, we cannot heal anyone. However, when you are anointed with the Spirit of the LORD, then

He can heal through you. This reality is found in the New Testament as well. Acts 10:38 (KJV) states,

> How God anointed Jesus of Nazareth with the Holy Ghost and with power: who went about doing good, and healing all that were oppressed of the devil; for God was with Him.

God anoints with the Holy Spirit and with power to heal. We have just witnessed this taught in both the Old and New Testaments. The Son of God (who was also fully man) was anointed to heal; He is our example.

Well, by now, you might be guessing where I'm going with this. Just as the Bible is teeming with passages supporting God as the One who heals and there is healing through the Holy Spirit, we learn how we are healed back in the Old Testament. We are told about the coming Messiah and how our healing comes about in Isaiah 53:5 (KJV):

> But he *was* wounded for our transgressions, *he was* bruised for our iniquities: the chastisement for our peace *was* upon Him; and with his stripes we are healed.

This passage refers to Jesus's eventual suffering for our sake. Jesus endured beatings that He did not deserve but we did. Because Jesus took our punishment, we now stand clean and forgiven before the throne of judgment—God's wrath satisfied.

And in the New Testament, 1 Peter 2:24 (NKJV) says our healing comes by Jesus:

> Who Himself bore our sins in His own body on the tree, that we, having died to sins, might live for righteousness—by whose stripes you were healed.

This eternal healing is offered to everyone. This is the Father's love for us. In Matthew 8:3 (KJV), after having come to Jesus worshipping Him, a leper asked Jesus if He was willing to heal him, and Jesus reached out His hand, touching him, saying,

> "I will; be thou clean." And immediately his leprosy was cleansed.

Powerful statements indeed! You and I are healed because Christ bore our sin. This is the good news of the Bible, folks. No other religion comes close. It is not by works. It is not because you are a good person—because no one is good enough, and no one is too rotten for Jesus. It is because the Son of God, God in the flesh, took off His heavenly crown and came down from heaven to enter time and space. Jesus, the Son of God, became a man and lived a perfect, sinless life. He became our propitiation (appeasement) and the sacrifice for our sin. No matter where we are at in life, all we have to do is say, "Yes, Lord, I believe in You and ask You to forgive me." It does not get any easier than that.

Jesus even said it was easy in Matthew 11:30 (KJV):

> For my yoke *is* easy, and my burden is light.

In both the Gospel of Matthew (written to Jews) and Luke (written to Gentiles), we are told numerous times of who on earth has the power and authority to heal.

In Matthew 8:6 (NKJV), a centurion comes to Jesus and tells Him,

> Lord, my servant is lying at home paralyzed, dreadfully tormented.

To which Jesus replies in Matthew 8:7 (NKJV),

> I will come and heal him.

I really like this short verse. You will notice Jesus does not say that he will go to his Father and ask Him to heal the servant. Nope. He does not say, "I will heal him by the Spirit" either. In radical form, Jesus says, "I will come and heal him." He said this with undeniable authority!

In Matthew 8:16 (NLT), we have Jesus casting out demons and healing:

> That evening many demon-possessed peo-
> ple were brought to Jesus. He cast out the evil
> spirits with a simple command, and he healed all
> the sick.

Next, Luke 4:40 (NKJV) says concerning Jesus,

> When the sun was setting, all those who had
> any that were sick with various diseases brought
> them to Him; and He laid His hands on every
> one of them and healed them.

What a gracious Lord we have. God does not run out of power. It says that "He laid His hands on every one of them and healed them." So He didn't just heal one or two; Jesus placed His hands on all of them who needed healing, and all were made well.

I'd like to wrap this up with Romans 8:2 (NKJV) as it relates to both Christ and the Spirit's equal partnership with respect to eternal healing. As the apostle Paul says,

> For the law of the Spirit of life in Christ
> Jesus has made me free from the law of sin and
> death.

We can understand that

- it is God who heals.
- we are healed through the Holy Spirit.

- Jesus heals.
- we are healed eternally by His (Jesus's) stripes.

A final thought: We do read of Jesus's disciples healing many, but remember, it is only as Jesus gave them power (Matthew 10:1) and commanded them in Matthew 10:5 to go out and

> Heal the sick, cleanse the lepers, raise the dead, cast out devils: freely ye have received, freely give. (Matthew 10:8 KJV)

If Jesus commanded them to heal, then He is the one providing the ability and power to do so. So cool—I don't need to add to it.

CHAPTER 5

e3

WHO DO WE WORSHIP?

In both Exodus and Deuteronomy, we see what is commonly referred to as the Ten Commandments. This is where Moses came down from Mount Sinai, having been given two tablets of stone by God to deliver to His people (Deuteronomy 4:13). The first three commandments are directed at our relationship with God. The first, I'm paraphrasing, is that we should not have any other god before our God. God demands to be first in our lives. God does not want our boat, our car, spouse, children, or job to be number one in our lives. HE wants to be number one. The first commandment states what God wants most from us—our hearts!

The second commandment is like the first—prioritizing our relationship with God as primary concern. Our God is a jealous God, and He commands us not to bow down and worship any other god but HIM. HE wants to be worshiped. HE says in Exodus 34:14 (KJV),

> For thou shalt worship no other god: for the
> LORD, whose name *is* Jealous, *is* a jealous God.

He is jealous for us with a selfless, passionate love. He knows that only His love in our lives will completely satisfy us. This is why in Deuteronomy 5:9 (NKJV), God is absolute in His command as it says,

> You shall not bow down to them nor serve them. For I, the LORD your God, *am* a jealous God.

"Them" is referring to any carved or handmade image. Of course, bowing down to anything is to worship it, and God detests this! We are commanded in the "Pentateuch," "Torah," or first five books of the Bible not to worship anything or anyone other than God. As we continue through the Old Testament, we are told in 2 Kings 17:36 (NLT),

> But worship only the LORD, who brought you out of Egypt with great strength and a powerful arm. Bow down to him alone, and offer sacrifices only to him.

This is compelling. We are not only called to worship God, but also to fear Him. The fear of the LORD here means to have great reverence for Him.

Psalm 86:9 (NLT) says concerning worship:

> All the nations You made will come and bow before you, Lord; they will praise your holy name.

Gotta love this! All the nations, or it could have said "the *whole world*," will come before the Lord to worship and glorify His Name. We see more about worship in Psalm 95:6–7 (NKJV):

> Oh come, let us worship and bow down;
> Let us kneel before the LORD our Maker. For He

is our God, And we *are* the people of His pasture,
And the sheep of His hand.

Though we want to stick to the chapter's heading about who we worship, we need to mention something here. When you get real with your faith and you make it practical, which means getting into the Word often, doing a personal study of Scripture, or attending Bible study at your church, words and phrases of God's triune nature will begin to pop out at you. Let's see what popped out to me just now.

As I had said a couple of chapters ago concerning the Spirit that Jesus said in both John 10:11 and 14 that He was the good shepherd, it may not have meant that much to you then; but when you put John 10:11 and 14 together with Psalm 95:6–7 (above). it changes our understanding of God and the unity He has with the Son and the Spirit. The psalmist is referring to our maker and shepherd as LORD, and in the book of John, we (believers) are sheep of the "good shepherd," Jesus. But not only that, we are the sheep of "His hand" too! Get it? There is a consistency in the Word of God. This consistent message brings Jesus the Son and God the Father together as one. The Holy Spirit helps us to understand this oneness between God the Father and Jesus the Son.

Now, let's look to the New Testament in Romans 14:11 (NKJV) and see who it is that demands to be worshipped:

> For it is written: *"As I live," says the* LORD,
> *"Every knee shall bow to Me, and every tongue shall*
> *confess to God."*

All or everyone will worship God. God does not deny Himself or HIS Word. There is an old saying to do something "the easy way or the hard way." For Christians, it will be a delight to bow our collective knees to God and confess Him as our sovereign Lord. As for nonbelievers, bowing and confessing God will come at a cost—they will be forced to bow because God's judgment will demand it! We know this because the verse before, in Romans 14:10, says that we will all stand before Christ's judgment seat.

Onward we go. You've most likely heard of the wise men—the magi or kings who visited the baby Jesus. There is a lot of conjecture as to who they were, and to be honest, no one knows for sure. Scripture says that they came from the East in Matthew 2:1. We don't know much about them, but we can guess that they were educated because they were considered to be priests, kings, astronomers, or magicians. All these titles refer to different areas of study and were acquired by men of education and status. These wise men follow the star from the East in Matthew 2:2 (KJV), saying,

> Where is he that is been born King of the
> Jews? For we have seen his star in the east, and are
> come to worship him.

Powerful prophecy! They came to worship Jesus—Jesus alone. Their sights were on the One who was born King of the Jews. This happened when King Herod was on the throne. The Bible says that when Herod found out about the Messiah's birth, he was "troubled." Truthfully, anyone in Herod's position might be concerned as he thought his own throne and power would become compromised. Herod gathered together his priests and scribes to ask them where the Christ was supposed to be born. They told Herod that He would be born in Bethlehem according to Scripture. The wise men reached the place of where Jesus was born, which was under the star they followed (Matthew 2:9). When they arrived at the house where Jesus was, Matthew 2:11 (KJV) defines their actions:

> And when they were come into the house,
> they saw the young child with Mary his mother,
> and fell down, and worshiped him: and when
> they had opened their treasures, they presented
> unto him gifts; gold, and frankincense, and
> myrrh.

So they worshiped the young Jesus, and after they had presented their gifts of gold, frankincense, and myrrh to the new King, the wise men were warned in a dream not to return to see Herod. Their dream instructed them to go back to their own country as Herod sought to kill the Christ. This is a wonderfully *true* story of our Lord Jesus's kingship and sovereignty.

Further, in the book of Matthew, we find Satan trying to tempt Jesus by offering Him all the worldly kingdoms if only Jesus would bow down and worship him, to which Jesus replied in Matthew 4:10 (NKJV),

> Then Jesus said to him, "Away with you, Satan! For it is written, '*You shall worship the* LORD *your God, and Him only you shall serve.*'"

Agreed and amen. We have just read that Jesus was worshiped as a child. Now Jesus as an adult tells Satan that we are to worship only the LORD our God and to serve Him only. As Christians, we get this. Jesus is God incarnate—human.

The Holy Spirit will be directing you to see the Father and Son as One. As Jesus states in John 4:23 (ESV),

> But the hour is coming, and is now here, when the true worshipers will worship the Father in spirit and truth, for the Father is seeking such people to worship him.

Do you see the Trinity? Ask the Lord to give you the Spirit of truth as Jesus instructed his followers in John 16:13 (ESV):

> When the Spirit of truth comes, he will guide you into all the truth, for he will not speak on his own authority, but whatever he hears he will speak, and he will declare to you the things that are to come.

These words are of great comfort. They are written to us and for us. We don't have to be inhibited concerning the Lord. Go to God, and tell Him that you don't get it or you don't understand. He will not let you down but will reveal His divine truth to you in remarkable ways.

Before you study the Word, ask the Lord for guidance and discernment. Too often, we (myself included) do it alone reading His Word. Keep in mind He is a big God, and we can only understand Him and the Word by and through His Holy Spirit. Sometimes I'll sit in bed reading the Bible and forget to pray beforehand. After reading, sometimes an entire chapter, I will sit back and think to myself, *What did I just read? I didn't understand a thing.* My mind will drift. So I'll pray, "Lord, by Your Spirit, give me wisdom and grace so that I can understand what it is about this scripture that You'd like me to know." Then I will read the chapter again, and instantly, some word or scripture will stick out to me. His Holy Spirit will direct me to His sovereign truth or some word of encouragement that I have been needing—absolutely awesome!

When I talk to cult members or new believers about the Trinity, I like to bring up the book of Hebrews. Though we are not sure who wrote it, this book of God still made it into our hands. One good guess is that Hebrews came from Paul's pen. The first chapter of Hebrews addresses the triune nature between the Father and the Son. God appoints Jesus as heir to all things. Hebrews 1:1-2 (NKJV) says that it was through Him (the Son) that

> God, who at various times and in various ways spoke in time past to the fathers by the prophets, has in these last days spoken to us by *His* Son, whom he appointed heir of all things, through whom also He made the worlds.

Hebrews 1:3 says that Jesus is the expressed *image of God* and that it is He Who upholds all things by the word of His power. That's pretty amazing—and as if that's not enough, God calls Him (Jesus) God! Yes, you read correctly. In Hebrews 1:8 (NLT), He says,

> But to the Son he says, "Your throne, O God, endures forever and ever. You rule with a scepter of justice."

So just to be clear, the Bible says that God calls Jesus God. God the Father also says in Hebrews 1:6 concerning the Firstborn (Jesus) (KJV),

> And let all the angels of God worship him.

Is that confusing? Of course not. God tells the angels to worship Jesus! Just this morning, I sat at a table in Starbucks with my Bible study brothers, discussing this very topic. I am blessed to be surrounded by guys who understand the Trinity and help me to stay grounded in the Word.

With worship in mind, I'd like to share just a few more verses about who we worship. One is in the book of John and the other two are in Revelation, the last book of the Bible. In John chapter 9, we read of a man who was blind from birth. Jesus's disciples inquired of Him if it was the man's or his parents' sin that caused him to be born blind. In John 9:3 (NKJV), we find,

> Jesus answered, "Neither this man nor his parents sinned, but that the works of God should be revealed in him."

What happened at this time was the healing of the man born blind. So Jesus spits on the ground, makes a little bit of mud, and applies it to the blind man's eyes. Then He tells the man to go wash in the "Pool of Siloam." When the blind man had done what Jesus told him to do, he came back to Jesus seeing! Later the previously blind man was questioned by the Pharisees because they did not believe his story. They also questioned his parents and ended up finding fault with Jesus because He had healed their son on the Sabbath. After having been cast out of the synagogue, Jesus found the formerly blind man who could now see and asked him in John 9:35 (NKJV),

Do you believe in the Son of God?

The man asked who it was so that he could believe in him (John 9:37 ESV).

And Jesus said to him, "You have seen him, and it is he who is speaking to you."

This is the good part. The once-blind man had a change of heart and realized Who it was that healed him when he said in John 9:38 (ESV),

"Lord, I believe," and he worshiped him.

The man worshiped Jesus! If we are only to worship God (and Jesus knew this with the temptation from Satan), then why didn't Jesus stop him from worshipping Him? He didn't need to because Jesus is God.

Wrapping things up, we are told who it is that gets worshiped in heaven. Revelation 4:10–11 (NKJV), speaking of the elders who surround the throne of God, says that,

The twenty-four elders fall down before Him who sits on the throne and worship Him who lives forever and ever, and cast their crowns before the throne, saying: "You are worthy, O Lord, To receive glory and honor and power; for You created all things, And by Your will they exist and were created."

This is—or should be—of paramount consideration for us as believers. Do you know what we are going to be doing in heaven?

Worshiping God! Now before you think this mundane and boring, wait. Do you think we serve a boring God? No way! Jesus, while on the cross with two other criminals, was asked by one of the criminals (Luke 23:42), "Lord, remember me when You come into Your kingdom," to which Jesus, knowing the man's change of heart, tells him in Luke 23:43 (NLT),

> I assure you, today you will be with me in paradise.

That sounds pretty cool to me. I want to spend eternity in His paradise!

Lastly, in Revelation 14:6–7 (NKJV),

> Then I saw another angel flying in the midst of heaven, having the everlasting gospel to preach to those who dwell on the earth—to every nation, tribe, tongue and people—saying with a loud voice, "Fear God and give glory to Him, for the hour of His judgment has come; and worship Him who made heaven and earth, the sea and springs of water."

I love that the Bible teaches we are to worship Jesus in heaven, but if you are thinking, *Didn't he just say a moment ago that'd we be worshiping God in heaven?* Yes, he did. That is because They are one and the same. Who do you think made heaven and earth? God, of course, but we will dig into that in the chapter on Creator.

I hope that His triune nature is becoming clear; there is a lot to take in. God is complex, and I'm glad He is. He wouldn't be much of a God if He were not deeper than we could understand. In this chapter, *we learned*:

- We only worship God.
- All nations (people) will worship the Lord and glorify His name.

- All creation will worship Him.
- Men worshiped the baby Jesus, the Messiah.
- Jesus said to worship the Lord God and only serve Him.
- True worshipers worship the Father in spirit and truth.
- God calls Jesus God.
- God tells the angels of God to worship Jesus.

CHAPTER 6

❦

THE FIRST AND THE LAST

I can't help it. Whenever I see "*the First and the Last*," I think of a race. It is an appropriate thought. In any race, there is one who finishes first and one who finishes last. I think of God this way, and it helps with my understanding of Him—that is to say He is the First, preeminent among everything. He "was" before time and, indeed, will "be" after time. He does not change. His being the Last means that after the race or when everything is done, He still "is." He is completely sovereign from the beginning to the end. The very first sentence of the very first book of the Bible (Genesis 1:1 KJV) proclaims,

> In the beginning God created the heaven
> and the earth.

This statement implies He already existed before the beginning. It does not say, "In the beginning God was made, and then He created everything else." Nope, it is and was He alone who started time and space then created. The implication is the same for Christ Jesus as well. We also established that Jesus was with God the Father before time (John 17:5). In John 17:24 (NKJV), Jesus even claims that God the Father loved Him before the world was:

> For You loved Me before the foundation of
> the world.

Both God the Father and Jesus the Son are both co-eternal and co-creator. Both are also before the beginning and after the end. This is important to understand because we are now going to see who it is that carries the title of the First and the Last. In Isaiah, we are first introduced to this title of God. Concerning Israel, God speaks of His help and power in this fashion as we read in Isaiah 41:4 (NLT),

> Who has done such mighty deeds, sum-
> moning each new generation from the beginning
> of time? It is I, the Lord, the First and the Last. I
> alone am he.

He constantly was reassuring Israel of His help and guidance. Israel was in rebellion and not obeying the Lord. Again, in Isaiah 44:6 (KJV), God says,

> Thus saith the Lord the King of Israel, and
> his redeemer the Lord of hosts; "I *am* the first,
> and I *am* the last; and beside me *there is* no God."

God said this after having just told His people that He formed them from the womb (Isaiah 44:2). God went on in Isaiah 44:3–4 to say that He would pour water on him who is thirsty and bless their offspring so much that they would spring up among the grass. What a great God and Father!

Finally, Isaiah 48:12 (NKJV) says,

> Listen to Me, O Jacob, And Israel, My
> called: I *am* He, I *am* the First, I *am* also the Last.

This is significant. This title of God is powerful, pivotal, and even paramount to our understanding of Him. Before there was anything—God. After everything—God. God has this great plan to redeem Israel (and us too), but they were constantly falling back into idolatry and disobeying His commands. God's restraint is obvious too. In Isaiah 49:9 and 11, God says that He will defer His anger and that He would do it for His own sake. Then He goes on to clarify Who He is in Isaiah 48:13 (NKJV):

> Indeed My hand has laid the foundation of
> the earth, And My right hand has stretched out
> the heavens.

There is no mistaking His sovereign rule.

We will now take a look into future events in the end times in the New Testament book of Revelation. No book garners more attention than Revelation. It is full of symbolism and end-times judgment. Revelation, as you know, is the last book of the Bible. It is in Revelation that you should find ample observational evidence to secure your trust and confidence in who the First and the Last is. I hope you make the connection just like the thief on the cross next to Jesus did. Revelation presents Jesus as Lord, Savior God, and King, your Redeemer, and your everlasting Father.

Starting with Revelation 1:11 (KJV), we are told by John that he was in the Spirit when he heard a loud voice behind him like a trumpet:

> Saying, "I am Alpha and Omega, the first
> and the last."

Right out of the gate in the first chapter of Revelation, we are already hearing about the First and the Last. Great news for us because John is going to let us in on what God looks like. Before we take a look at HIM, you may be thinking, *Isn't God invisible?* My answer is a resounding yes. However, in Colossians 1:15 (NKJV), referring to Jesus Christ the Son, it says,

> He is the image of the invisible God, the firstborn over all creation.

You read that correctly. Pretty amazing, I know. I have a hard time wrapping my head around it too. God is invisible, yet Jesus, the Son of God, is the image of God Himself. Now before you question the whole "*firstborn*" thing, like so many do, we need to understand that to be called the firstborn meant "inheritor" or one who would have authority over things. We have already seen that Jesus does have this authority. Just to note, in Psalm 89, God says about King David in verse 27 (KJV) that

> Also I will make him my firstborn, higher than the kings of the earth.

Interesting that God would call David His firstborn because David was the youngest in his family, having eight older brothers. By saying this, in essence, God was declaring that David would be king and inherit God's earthly throne. Jesus the Son will also inherit the throne, but His will be eternal, from everlasting to everlasting.

Let's go back to Revelation. The apostle John turns around to see who it was that was talking to him and then describes the First and the Last in detail. Reading from Revelation 1:13-15 (ESV),

> And in the midst of the lampstands one like a son of man, clothed with a long robe and with a golden sash around his chest. The hairs of his head were white, like white wool, like snow. His eyes were like a flame of fire, his feet were like burnished bronze, refined in a furnace, and his voice was like the roar of many waters.

This is none other than King Jesus, our King, and I appreciate what follows. The Bible says that when John saw Him (Revelation 1:17 ESV),

> I fell at His feet as though dead.

Amen—I think we all would have. If John were not in the Spirit, as he said he was, he would have died. As the Bible also says, no one can see God's face and live (Exodus 33:20).

As we have read about the First and the Last thus far, it has been pretty cut and dry that it is the LORD God we are talking about. Not so with what follows. After the Lord puts His hand on John and told him to not be afraid, He tells John in Revelation 1:17–18 (NKJV),

> I am the First and the Last. I am He who lives, and was dead, and behold, I am alive for-evermore. Amen. And I have the keys of Hades and of Death.

This really gets me! I had to read this, I think, three times. The First and the Last, God, was dead and now is alive? Did God ever die and come back to life? No, but we know Jesus did.

Admittedly, these verses cinched the deal for me. Many years ago, when I was looking this stuff up, I couldn't believe what I was reading. Growing up Catholic, I didn't do much reading or studying on the triune nature of God. As a teen, I remember asking the Lord to show Himself to me in His Word. This was about the time that I made the decision to follow Jesus Christ—when I read this passage in Revelation 1. There was no aha moment, no bright light, and no choir of angels singing. I just remember thinking, *Okay, I get it now—Jesus is God.* I sincerely hope that this truth is finding its way into your heart as it did mine. Nothing is better than coming to know the truth of who Jesus is and allowing the peace of His truth to conquer your life. You will never experience a more perfect peace than His.

Next, we hear the Lord telling John to write to the church of Smyrna. Smyrna is one of the seven churches mentioned in the book of Revelation. Here the Lord gives His Name again. Revelation 2:8 (NLT) says,

> Write this letter to the angel of the church in Smyrna. This is the message from the one who is the First and the Last, who was dead but is now alive.

So, who is He talking about this time—Lazarus, maybe? Nope, not even close. I say this jokingly because Jesus did raise a man named Lazarus, who, when he had died, Jesus brought him back to life (John 11). No, this passage in Revelation is not Lazarus but our glorified Lord Jesus Christ, the Messiah, the Son of God, the King of kings and Lord of lords. It is fitting that God's revealing of Himself reaches a pinnacle of sorts here in Revelation. Throughout both testaments, there are several descriptions and titles of God. He has revealed to us that He is Creator, Savior, Redeemer, and God the Son. I could go on for another page or so, but you get the idea. In the last chapter (Revelation 22:12), the Lord says,

> And, behold, I come quickly; and my reward is with me, to give every man according as his work shall be.

Not that we deserve it, but is that not great news? We get a reward! We each know what we deserve and what we should get. It is amazing that though our God is a judge, He is also a God of grace and shows mercy toward each of us. Thank You, Jesus! So His reward is with Him, and He says this just before qualifying Himself again in Revelation 22:13 (KJV),

> I am Alpha and Omega, the Beginning and the end, the first and the last.

I love this. No guesswork here. There is only one Alpha and Omega, and He is the Almighty (Revelation 1:8). There is only one Beginning and one End, Who gives of the fountain of the water of life (Revelation 21:6). There is only one First and Last, Who is Redeemer and God (Isaiah 44:6).

As the passage goes on, we are told that those who do His commandments are blessed. Those on the outside of the gates of His city are the sexually immoral, murderers, idolaters, and those that practice lying (Revelation 22:14-15), and I share this because I want you to know who it is that is saying all this. Who is calling Himself the First and the Last is revealed in the very next verse, Revelation 22:16 (KJV):

> I Jesus have sent mine angel to testify unto you these things in the churches. I am the root and the Offspring of David, and the bright and morning star.

We now know that

- God is the First and the Last.
- Jesus is the First and the Last.
- the First and the Last was dead but alive forevermore.

CHAPTER 7

৩

THE I AM

When God sent Moses to Pharaoh in Egypt (Exodus 3:10) to deliver the children of Israel from the hand of Pharaoh, Moses told the people (verse 13 NKJV) that their God had sent him to them, and when they responded by asking, "What's His name?" God told Moses to respond by saying, "I Am Who I Am" (Exodus 3:14 ESV). Remarkable!

No other name garners more regard than the One we call the Great I Am. This name is unique to God only and suits only Him. When we use the term "I am" (regarding ourselves), we always use it in conjunction with something else. We may say "I am an excellent baseball player" or "I am an accountant." However, only God says it in the demonstrative sense. Only He can say I Am without adding anything to it. This I Am name and how it identifies God appears about three hundred times in the Bible. From Genesis of the Old Testament to Revelation of the New Testament, we find that the name "I Am" is both synonymous with God the Father and God the Son, Jesus Christ.

Starting in Genesis 15:1b (NKJV), in a vision to Abram, the Lord says,

> I am your shield, your exceedingly great reward.

Certainly, this is wonderful news that the God of the universe calls Himself our shield. In times of hardship, we should keep this verse in mind—God is our protector, our shield, and always is looking out for our best interest. Though Jesus is not mentioned as being our shield, it is important to recognize that our salvation is dependent upon our trust and belief in Him. Even Jesus said in John 14:1 (NKJV),

You believe in God, believe also in Me.

Our next verse comes from the book of Isaiah 43:13 (KJV). This particular verse lets us know that God is outside of time:

Yea, before the day *was* I *am* he.

This is a distinct quality of God. Indeed, before time, He was. This revealing of His omnipresence is what we have already discovered to be one of His identities as the First and the Last. Looking at chapter 43 verse 25 (KJV) to see who it is that forgives sin,

I, even I, am He who blots out your transgressions for My own sake; and I will not remember your sins.

The best news ever! Not only is God the one who forgives our sin, but when we make that conscious decision to believe in Him and trust in Him as our Savior, He does not even remember our sin. This authority to forgive is demonstrated with Jesus in Luke 7:48 as well. God's ability not to remember our sin may be difficult to understand because how could an all-powerful God not remember or forget our sin? Simply put, God does not forget anything, but HE does choose not to remember our sin or bring it up again. Keep in mind HE paid for all of our sin when we came to HIM and repented. Jesus paid our debt on the cross and said "*tetelestai*," which means "paid in full." Interesting because back around Jesus's time, this was a Greek phrase that would be written on a bill when something was paid for, and it was also one of the last things Jesus said when He was crucified.

The next scripture we'll look at comes from the book of Isaiah. In chapter 43 verse 15 (NKJV), we are told by the LORD our Redeemer,

> I *am* the LORD, your Holy One, the Creator
> of Israel, your King.

Again a powerful statement because it is a verse that unveils God's triune nature. We know this because Jesus Himself is called the Holy One in Mark 1:24 and King in Matthew 2:2 of the New Testament.

The last verse we'll look at comes from the book of Genesis in 28:15 (NKJV), where in a dream, God speaks to Jacob and says,

> Behold, I *am* with you and will keep you
> wherever you go, and will bring you back to this
> land.

This is not just another promise to Jacob, but this is a promise from God to all believers. Our God is without equal, and He will never leave us or forsake us—praise God!

In the New Testament, we find Jesus being led into the council of both the chief priests and scribes after having been beaten, and they inquire in Luke 22:70 (NKJV), saying,

> Are You then the Son of God?

To which Jesus replies,

> You *rightly* say that I am.

By agreeing with them that He was the Son of God, Jesus was saying not only was He equal with God but that He was God in the flesh. To the Pharisees, priests, and scribes, this was blasphemy and deserving of death and why they sought to kill Him.

Jesus goes on to make several other comparisons between Himself and the Father in the New Testament.

In John chapter 8, Jesus is speaking to the Jews about believers having immortality, and they bring up that Abraham is dead (verse 52), and Jesus responds (verse 56 ESV):

> Your father Abraham rejoiced that he would
> see my day. He saw it and was glad.

This really angered the Jews because they knew what Jesus was implying. We can understand this by what they said next. They came back to Jesus in verse 57 (ESV):

> You are not yet fifty years old, and have you
> seen Abraham?

And here is the good part—drumroll, please! Jesus says the most radical thing in history in verse 8:58 (ESV):

> Truly, truly, I say to you, before Abraham
> was, I am.

He just told the Jews again that He was, indeed, God! So they reward Him by picking up rocks (verse 59) to throw at Him, but Jesus hid Himself. What we can also take away from the preceding verse is that of Jesus's own claim of omnipresence is just like that of the Father.

So, we have just read two great references pointing to Jesus and God the Father as being the I am. As I have said, this continuity of the Father and Son is taught throughout the whole Bible.

When talking to His disciples concerning the way, Jesus's disciple Thomas says, "How can we know the way?" And Jesus responds in John 14:6 (KJV):

> I am the way, the truth, and the life: no man
> cometh unto the Father, but by me.

Here Jesus is revealing that He is one and the same as God. We can back up His claim when we read Isaiah 65:16 (KJV), which says, *"the God of truth."* So, both God the Father and Jesus the Son claim to be truth, and that's not all. In Romans 8:10 (KJV), we know that it says "the Spirit *is* life." By saying what He did, Jesus was exposing His triune nature again. The interrelation of God's Holy Trinity strengthens at every verse. Mirroring God's claim to never leave us is Jesus's words to His disciples in Galilee, where He says in Matthew 28:20 (KJV) comfortingly,

> And, lo, I am with you always, even unto
> the end of the world. Amen.

Here Jesus makes the same claim as that of the Father. The only other personage in the Bible with this kind of authority is the Holy Spirit, who is called the Helper or Comforter. In John 14:16 (NKJV), Jesus says that He will pray to the Father and that He would send *"another Helper, that He may abide with you forever."* Even in Ephesians 1:13 we are told that we would be sealed by the Holy Spirit of promise. Lastly, Jesus makes a claim as to His messianic kingship when He speaks from Revelation 22:16 (NKJV), saying,

> I am the Root and the Offspring of David,
> the Bright and Morning Star.

I am particularly fond of this scripture because not only does it speak of Christ's humanity in the flesh, but it is also prophecy being fulfilled where the blessed line of the Messiah is confirmed from Genesis 49:10 (NLT):

> The scepter will not depart from Judah.

What we know about God the Father, Jesus the Son, and the Holy Spirit:

- God is the I AM.
- Jesus is the I am.

Chapter 8

— ❧ —

The Creator

Perhaps the most common and well-received name or title of God is that of being called Creator. Indeed, from the first book of the Bible and in the first verse in Genesis chapter 1:1 (NLT), we are told,

> In the beginning God created the heavens
> and the earth.

That's simple enough. Certainly, the ultimate power and authority in the universe designed and created us. I believe this is the first thing mentioned in the Bible because it is the preeminent object that brings God glory and honor. Before time—God. Before a physical universe—God. Then God created. There are several verses that proclaim God's divine and glorious creation, so let's continue as we have first with Old Testament then onto the New Testament.

In Isaiah 40, we are treated to a wonderful account of God's omniscient being. This chapter reveals He is caring, all-knowing, His strength and power. In verse 28 (NKJV) we read,

> Have you not known? Have you not heard?
> The everlasting God, the Lord, the Creator of the
> ends of the earth, neither faints nor is weary.

It is difficult for me to understand that someone or something cannot run out of power or lose steam and become fatigued, but that is our God. He does not tire and His power is infinite and thank Him for it. Our universe is so vast; I can't imagine the chaos that would ensue if the billions of galaxies out there were not in His proverbial hands. With Nehemiah 9:6 (NLT) we are told who it is that made heaven:

> You alone are the Lord. You made the skies
> and the heavens and all the stars.

Again simple enough. In Psalm 50, God declares His sovereign ownership over all the animals as verse 11 (NLT) says,

> I know every bird on the mountains, and all
> the animals of the field are Mine.

God owns everything, and when we read of Him professing ownership, it is because He designed and created all things. And speaking of His everlasting mercy and creation, we read in Psalm 136:5, 6 (NLT):

> Give thanks to him who made the heavens
> so skillfully. His faithful love endures forever.
> Give thanks to him who placed the earth among
> the waters.

This is truly wonderful—reading these verses that extol God's loving grace and creation. The last scripture we'll look at from the Old Testament, again, comes from the book of Isaiah. If there could possibly be any doubt as to who our Creator is, here God plainly tells us in chapter 44, verse 24 (NKJV),

> Thus says the Lord, your Redeemer, and
> He who formed you from the womb: "I am the
> Lord, who makes all things, Who stretches out

the heavens all alone, Who spreads abroad the earth by Myself."

So, no misunderstanding that, right? God boldly declares that HE is the Creator who made everything. This is what makes our God so personal and loving. HE is intricately involved in every aspect of HIS creation. As per the norm, let's jump into the New Testament and read who it is there who creates.

In the Gospel of John (of Christ's deity), we are informed as to who the Word is. Starting in John 1:1–2 (NKJV), we read,

> In the beginning was the Word, and the Word was with God, and the Word was God. He was in the beginning with God.

This is intriguing because who was God, and who could possibly be around with God from the beginning? Well, we are told Who it is in the next verse as John 1:3 (NKJV) says,

> All things were made through Him, and without Him nothing was made that was made.

This verse is speaking about the incarnate Lord Jesus Christ before He was physically born. We know this because it says about the Word in John 1:14 (NKJV):

> And the Word became flesh and dwelt among us, and we beheld His glory, the glory as of the only begotten of the Father, full of grace and truth.

This is a dynamic display of God's triune power at work. Very distinctly, we can understand that God, who has no physical form, became a physical man as the Son of God. Magnificent! We can better relate to this when we take a look into the book of Hebrews—presumably written by the apostle Paul. In Hebrews 1:3 (KJV), we are told concerning the Son,

> Who being the brightness of his glory, and the express image of his person, and upholding all things by the word of his power, when he had by himself purged our sins, sat down on the right hand of the Majesty on high.

This too is a lot to take in. Now we can see that it is Jesus who upholds all things and that He is the image of the personage of God. We can further see this in the book of Colossians, also written by Paul. We are told in Colossians 1:15 (KJV) about Jesus:

> Who is the image of the invisible God, the firstborn of every creature.

And though this helps with our understanding of who Jesus is, as we have read this before, it is really the next verse that identifies Him as the Creator. We read in chapter 1, verse 16 (NKJV):

> For by Him all things were created that are in heaven and that are on earth, visible and invisible, whether thrones or dominions or principalities or powers. All things were created through Him and for Him.

Here we get a complete description of Jesus as Creator of the universe and as the omnipotent God. He not only made the material universe, but He made heaven, the angels, and the throne of God as well.

So, we have covered enough ground to understand that it is God the Father and Jesus the Son that are both co-Creators. But does the Bible mention the Spirit as Creator? Indeed, it does. As we have discovered, not every title or name of God is mentioned with all *three* personages of the godhead. Remember, it is not the Spirit's job to bring glory to Himself but to direct that Glory to God the Father and the Lord Jesus Christ. However, in the book of Job, we are given a glimpse into the majesty of the Spirit of God, where we read chapter 33, verse 4 (KJV):

> The Spirit of God hath made me, and the
> breath of the Almighty hath given me life.

Here, Job's friend Elihu addresses him and his present condition of suffering. What is interesting is that Elihu seems to be the only friend of Job's who's got the right answer. He tells Job that his suffering isn't because God is judging him, but rather, that there must be some underlying reason for it—and there most certainly was! I don't want to spoil the story of Job, but Job's suffering was an example for the ages. Elihu also tells Job to humble himself and repent.

When we seek God, the Spirit of truth is within us, and we can declare truth and God's glory as Elihu did.

In this chapter, we discovered that

- God is Creator.
- Jesus is Creator.
- The (Holy) Spirit is Creator.

CHAPTER 9

❧

THE LIGHT

We've read so far some of the names and titles of God such as the I Am, the Savior, and the First and the Last. We have also read about some of God's attributes—who heals and who is worshipped. I'd like to share now about what describes God's divine, radiant light and what is revealed about light, its nature, and who is Light.

Right from the beginning, in Genesis 1:4, God saw that the light (day) was good, and He divided the day (Genesis 1:5) and the darkness (night) as the first day. Already God calls light good, and *light* is used throughout the Bible as an illustration of following God, walking in righteousness, and/or the absence of sin. In Exodus 13:21 (NKJV), it is the Lord who leads the children of Israel through the wilderness:

> By night in a pillar of fire to give them light.

Again light is good. God leads His people this way for forty years in the wilderness. Where we see opposition to light, it is indicated as sin. In Job 24:13 (NLT),

> Wicked people rebel against the light. They
> refuse to acknowledge its ways or stay in its paths.

This verse points to the lack of moral discretion and the presence of sin.

Darkness is used to describe someone who is apart from God, living in sin. We can see this in 1 Samuel 2:9 (NKJV) as we read,

> He will guard the feet of His saints, but the
> wicked shall be silent in darkness.

Those not walking with the LORD are in darkness, but with believers, He will guide their steps—light their path.

In the book of Job, we to see the connection between light and the Lord. As Job 33:30 (NKJV) says,

> That he may be enlightened with the light
> of life.

Through Job's struggle, he is reconciled to God by God's promise of the coming Messiah—Jesus. This *"life"* is Jesus, and we know that Jesus is Life and the author of life. It is interesting that the Bible uses the word *enlightened* here to describe that relationship with the light of life because of how it is used in Hebrews of the New Testament. Hebrews 6:4 (NKJV) says,

> For it is impossible for those who were once
> enlightened, and have tasted the heavenly gift,
> and have become partakers of the Holy Spirit.

Here is another one of those verses that speaks of the trinity of God. I appreciate the relevance between the tasting of the heavenly gift (knowing Jesus) and the association with the Holy Spirit. That is to say knowing Jesus, believing in what He has done for us, and accepting Christ as our Savior is by the power of the Holy Spirit. Indeed, when we come to that point of understanding that it is all Jesus, we are truly partakers, having been enlightened by the Holy Spirit to the good news of redemption through Jesus Christ.

There are several other verses throughout the Old Testament that refer to God and Jesus the Messiah as the light. In Psalm 27:1 (KJV), speaking of God, King David says,

> The LORD is my light and my salvation;
> whom shall I fear?

A rhetorical question for sure, but Saul was always after David, wanting to kill him. Yet by this passage, we know that God was David's light. This is compelling too because God was also David's salvation—sounds like another chapter study.

And in Isaiah 60:20 (KJV), we see God described as light:

> For the LORD shall be thine everlasting light.

Lastly, light is associated with the coming Messiah in Isaiah 49:6 (NKJV):

> I will give You as a light to the Gentiles, that
> You should be My salvation to the ends of the
> earth.

Not only is this verse an example of God's triune nature, but it is also a prophetic one as well. Only the Bible contains fulfilled prophecy. We know this by the proceeding verses, which declare Him as the Redeemer of Israel and the Holy One of Israel.

In the New Testament's Gospel of Matthew, we are given a peek into Christ's radiant glory when He is transfigured before His disciples' eyes and met by Moses and Elijah in Matthew 17:2 (NLT):

> Jesus' appearance was transformed so that
> his face shone like the sun, and his clothes became
> as white as light.

I would have loved to have been there to see my Lord change to bright light before my eyes. Can you imagine what Peter, James, and

John must have thought? And how did the disciples seemingly know it was Moses and Elijah that were with Him? Were they wearing name tags? I don't know, but I really doubt it. I think the disciples got a glimpse of eternity that gave them a supernatural awareness that was both heavenly and holy. Certainly in the gracious presence of our glorified Lord, there must be a spiritual insight or awareness that is overwhelming.

In John 1:7 (NKJV), the author, presumably St. John, tells us of John the Baptist:

> This man came for a witness, to bear witness of the Light [Jesus], that all through him might believe.

And in case we aren't sure of who exactly we're talking about, the next verse, verse 8 (NKJV), says,

> He [John] was not that light, but was sent to bear witness of that light [Jesus].

I point this out to Muslims who believe John is saying that he was the light himself. When we read further, down to John 1:10 (NLT), we can clearly see who John describes as light can only be one person as we read,

> He came into the very world he created, but the world didn't recognize him.

Again the Creator Jesus revealed. Though not always easy to grasp, I have taken the liberty to use brackets in a couple of verses so that the new believer will understand who the Bible is talking about. The Gospel of John focuses on the deity of Christ Jesus, and it does not always reference Him by the name Jesus, but rather, *He* or *Him* is substituted. This may confuse a new believer.

Further into John 8:12 (NKJV), Jesus tells us directly who He is. Jesus describes Himself this way:

> I am the light of the world. He who follows Me shall not walk in darkness, but have the light of life.

Two things here: First, Jesus describes Himself as light; but also notice, if we are following Him, we are not in darkness, not walking in sin! Amen.

In the book of Acts, I believe we are treated to an example of God's appearance as a Christophany, a nonphysical manifestation of Jesus as Peter is in prison and chained between two soldiers when in Acts 12:7 (NKJV):

> Now behold, an angel of the Lord stood by him, and a light shone in the prison; and he struck Peter on the side and raised him up, saying, "Arise quickly!" And his chains fell off his hands.

This is awesome because this type of physical manifestation is not common in Scripture. We rarely read of any bodily form of God, Son of God, the Holy Spirit, or of angels. Seeing God's physical light in this way shows us just how involved He really is.

As mentioned before, the only other time I know of that we see this kind of manifestation of the Lord in the New Testament is when the Holy Spirit descended like a dove in Luke 3:22 and in Acts 22:6 (NKJV), where Saul, before he became Paul, was on the road to Damascus when

> Suddenly a great light from heaven shone around me.

Saul falls to the ground and hears a voice saying,

> SAUL, SAUL, why are you persecuting me?
> (Acts 22:7 NLT)

So Saul inquires, asking the Lord who it is that is speaking to him, and in Acts 22:8 (NKJV), we are told:

> I am Jesus of Nazareth, whom you are persecuting.

Such a powerful passage. Flat out, Jesus says it's Him! Remember too this meeting that Saul had with the Lord Jesus was after Jesus's own crucifixion. Jesus must have been in His glory. No wonder Saul said that the light came from heaven. I believe it was a manifestation of God's Shekinah glory light that Saul was seeing.

It is unmistakable if you are seeking the truth and not an argument or a loophole that both Jesus and God are light and that we are enlightened by His Spirit. You should like what comes next. In 2 Corinthians 4:4 (NKJV), we are told that

> The light of the gospel of the glory of Christ,
> who is the image of God, should shine on them.

Here again, Jesus is the image God and the light of the *good news* of the gospel. The gospel is all about believing in Jesus. We know too that God is Spirit and cannot be seen, but when we see Jesus, we are seeing the Father.

We'll wrap this up with just a couple more verses. In 1 John 1:5 (NLT), we read,

> God is light, and there is no darkness in him
> at all.

Right to the point—God is light, and there is no darkness (sin) in Him. This is the same message that we get from Jesus. Read on.

In Revelation 21:23 (NLT), this *light* doctrine is wrapped up as we are treated to a glimpse of what we will experience in heaven:

> And the city has no need of sun or moon,
> for the glory of God illuminates the city, and the
> Lamb [Jesus] is its light.

Fascinating for us believers. God Himself will illuminate heaven with the Lamb of God, who is Jesus, forever. Both God and Jesus are the light. Praise God!

We know that

- God is light.
- Jesus is the light of the world.

CHAPTER 10

❧

REDEEMER

Interestingly, in the New Testament, Jesus is never once called our redeemer. Yet in the Old Testament, God as Redeemer is mentioned some eighteen times. After cross-referencing Old and New Testament verses, we shall see an unmistakable parallel between God the Father, Jesus the Son, and the Holy Spirit as Redeemer.

As has been the standard, there are an abundance of verses proving the triune nature of the Redeemer in both Testaments, so we'll look at verses that share a connection in divine nature or essence of the three personages of God.

In Job, perhaps the oldest book of the Bible, we first read of a redeemer. We are told in chapter 19, verse 25 (KJV),

> For I know that my redeemer liveth, and
> *that he* shall stand at latter *day* upon the earth.

So the first time God is mentioned as Redeemer, it tells us that "He shall stand." Now we know that God has no corporeal body and that He is invisible, so who is it that stands? Well, we know that Jesus stood on the earth, and when He returns, Zechariah 14:4 tells us He will stand on the Mount of Olives. We also can denote the reference to Christ in Revelation 10:2 where Jesus will put his right foot on the sea and his left foot on the land. Indeed, it is the Lord Jesus who stands on the earth.

In Psalm 78:35 (KJV), we read again descriptions that relate equally to God the Father and the Lord Jesus:

> And they remembered that God *was* their rock, and the high God their redeemer.

It is important for us to understand that God does not share glory with anyone else—HE alone is omnipotent. When we see words like *rock* that are only used to describe God the Father or the Lord Jesus Christ, we can make the connection that what is being revealed here is God's triune nature. Some Catholics confuse the verbiage of *rock* being given as a name to the disciple Peter and say that the universal or Catholic church was built on him. This is a misnomer. Jesus did call Simon Bar-Jonah "*petros,*" meaning a small, movable stone or pebble; but when Jesus refers to Himself as a rock, He used the word *petra*—meaning a boulder or immovable rock or cliff. So in context, we can see that the church was never built on Peter but, rather, the Lord Jesus. If we have doubts about this, we can read just a little further into the book Matthew. In Matthew 16:21, Jesus tells His disciples that He will go to Jerusalem, be killed there, and rise on the third day. Well, this didn't sit well with Peter, so Peter takes the Lord aside and rebukes Him and says that it will never happen. Jesus turns to Peter and says,

> Get behind Me, Satan! (Matthew 16:23 NKJV)

Incredible, right? Jesus equating Peter with Satan. Actually, it was Peter's pride and mindset that He was rebuking. Jesus was speaking prophetically when He said that He would be killed—and we know who it is that condemns Scripture.

Next is what I'd call a nice lesson for Jehovah's Witnesses. They will point to Isaiah 9:6, where it says the Messiah is called "Mighty God" and say yes, He is called mighty god but not "Almighty" God, as it says in Genesis. When they bring this up, reducing Jesus's deity as to being merely God's son, a good verse to point them to is Proverbs 23:11 (KJV):

> For their redeemer is mighty; he shall plead
> their cause with thee.

You just cannot argue with Scripture—it is the undeniable truth. Here God is identified as "mighty." So sometimes God is called mighty in Scripture, and at other times HE is called almighty. He is still God.

If you remember, we had cross-referenced Jesus as being the King and the First and the Last in Isaiah 44:6 (ESV), but it also calls Him Redeemer in the same verse, so it bears repeating:

> Thus says the LORD, the King of Israel and
> his Redeemer, the LORD of hosts: "I am the first
> and I am the last; besides me there is no god."

That verse gets more powerful every time we read it—besides Him, there is no God. Amen!

As we have also mentioned before, both the Son and the Father are co-Creators, and this is made abundantly clear in Isaiah 44:24 (NKJV), where we read,

> Thus says the LORD, your Redeemer, and
> He who formed you from the womb: "I *am* the
> LORD, who makes all *things*, Who stretches out
> the heavens all alone, Who spreads abroad
> the earth by Myself."

This is fascinating for sure. God is so direct and so abundantly clear. HE tells us that HE formed (created) us and that HE made everything by HIMSELF—no help from anyone. With the next verse, the LORD shares a unique title that gives us another glimpse into the future and a future event. As said, we Christians who have put all our trust in the Lord will eventually one day become the collective bride of Christ as promised in Revelation. Here in Isaiah 54:5 (NKJV), HE lets us know:

> For your Maker *is* your husband, The LORD of hosts *is* His name; And your Redeemer *is* the Holy One of Israel; He is called the God of the whole earth.

It is not hard to see if we are truly seeking the truth in Scripture. Our Maker or Creator is our husband (Jesus), and HE not only is our Holy One, but HE is the One who made this planet we call Earth. As we have learned, both God and Jesus the Son are our Savior. Likewise, we read that They are both our Redeemer in Isaiah 60:16 (NLT):

> You will know at last that I, the Lord, am your Savior and your Redeemer, the Mighty One of Israel.

From the New Testament, in Galatians 5:22 (NKJV), we are told of the fruit of the Holy Spirit. For it says,

> The fruit of the Spirit is love, joy, peace, longsuffering, kindness, goodness, faithfulness, gentleness, self control. Against such there is no law.

When we are actively walking with the Lord, we receive these gifts, and our understanding of redemption matures. As Romans 8:23 (NKJV) says,

> But we also who have the firstfruits of the Spirit, even we ourselves groan within ourselves, eagerly waiting for the adoption, the redemption of our body.

Certainly our relationship with the Lord is blessed and nurtured when we mature as Christians and realize that the firstfruits of the Lord are both Jesus and the Spirit through whom we have been redeemed. Paul mentions this in both Romans and 1 Corinthians.

In Ephesians 4:30 (ESV), we are given an admonishment of sorts where we read,

> And do not grieve the Holy Spirit of God, by whom you were sealed for the day of redemption.

Distinctly, there is a connection to the reality of our being redeemed from sin and the Holy Spirit. It is the recognition as Christ as our Lord. Remember, the Spirit of wisdom gives us understanding and knowledge (Isaiah 11:2). Do not reject God's plan of salvation, and walk in a way that pleases Him.

Concerning our redemption through God the Son, Galatians 3:13 (ESV) declares,

> Christ has redeemed us from the curse of the law by becoming a curse for us-for it is written, "Cursed is everyone who is hanged on a tree."

Also, in Romans 3:24 (NKJV), it says of Jesus,

> Being justified freely by His grace through the redemption that is in Christ Jesus.

Lastly, we read in Ephesians 1:7 (ESV) that

> In Him we have redemption through his blood, the forgiveness of our trespasses, according to the riches of his grace.

Did God the Father ever bleed? Definitely not! But most assuredly, Jesus, the lamb of God, did. It is by the shedding of His blood that we have been set free and are redeemed.

We can now be comforted by knowing:

- God is our Redeemer.
- We are redeemed through the Spirit.
- Redemption is in Jesus.
- There is redemption through His blood.

CHAPTER 11

❧

SALVATION

Throughout this study, I have tried to repeatedly show how the Old and New Testament share a continuity of God's holy Word as it relates to the triune nature of God. With this final chapter study, I'd like to introduce our last title, Salvation. In the theological sense, salvation likely means the deliverance from sin and punishment. Indeed, God the Father has redeemed us through the Son, Jesus Christ, who is our salvation.

Starting in the Old Testament in Exodus, where God leads His people from slavery out of Egypt, we read in chapter 15, verse 2 (ESV),

> The Lord is my strength and my song, and
> He has become my salvation; this is my God, and
> I will praise him, my father's God, and I will exalt
> him.

What is appealing to me about this verse is the reoccurring adjectives that are used to describe God—reason being the same repeated words or phrases that describe the LORD (YAHWEH) are the same words and phrases that describe Jesus. As mentioned before, it is for this reason that I have purposely shared some of the same scripture in different chapters. Upon reading these scriptures, it should be of no wonder to us why the Bible teaches that both God the Father and Jesus the Son are our salvation. Another scripture that reveals who our salvation is comes from the book of 2 Samuel. In chapter 22, verse 47 (ESV) it reads,

> The Lord lives, and blessed be my rock, and
> exalted be my God, The rock of my salvation.

This scripture aligns perfectly with what we have already read in other books of the Bible. Again, God is our Rock just as Jesus is and our salvation. A reference about the coming Messiah in Psalm 21:5 (NKJV), presumably written by David, says,

> His glory is great in Your salvation; Honor
> and majesty You have placed upon him.

What is fascinating here is that David had a keen sense of God's identity. He understood that salvation came through God and that the coming Messiah King would have great glory, honor, and majesty and be, as Psalm 21:6 (NKJV) states,

> Most blessed forever.

So not only did David understand and trust in God and the coming Messiah, but he recognized that it was by God's Spirit that he would be upheld and saved as we read Psalm 51:12 (KJV),

> Restore unto me the joy of thy salvation;
> and uphold me *with thy free* spirit.

What makes this such a bold statement about salvation is its depth. David was called "a man after God's own heart," and it really shows in Scripture. In the preceding verse, verse 11 (NKJV), David pleads to God:

> Do not cast me away from Your presence,
> and do not take Your Holy Spirit from me.

It appears to me that David understands God to be a three-personage being. How else would he grasp God the Father, the Messiah King, and the work of the Holy Spirit? I believe when we truly give our hearts to the Lord, we are given insight into the eternal majesty of God.

With that, let's just read one more verse from the Old Testament. In the book of Zechariah, written sometime around the sixth century BC, the author, presumably Zechariah, writes of God's covenant relationship to His people. Here we are treated to one of the better or more obvious prophecies about the coming Messiah Jesus. In chapter 9, verse 9 (ESV), we are told,

> Rejoice greatly, O daughter of Zion! Shout aloud, O daughter of Jerusalem! Behold, your king is coming to you; righteous and having salvation is he, humble and mounted on a donkey, on a colt, the foal of a donkey.

This is so compelling! Zechariah is talking of the coming Messiah King over five hundred years before Jesus came, knowing that it is Jesus who brings salvation, the Savior of the world.

Come to the New Testament in the Gospel of Matthew, and we are treated to the fulfillment of Zechariah. In Matthew 21:2, we are told by Jesus as they came near to Jerusalem that He sent two of His disciples to go into a town and get a donkey and a colt that were tied together. In Matthew 21:5, we read Zechariah 9:9 almost verbatim; and in Matthew 21:7 we have the prophetic fulfillment of Matthew 21:5 (ESV)

> Say to the daughter of Zion, "Behold, your king is coming to you, humble, and mounted on a donkey, on a colt, the foal of a beast of burden."

and Matthew 21:7 (NKJV):

> They brought the donkey and the colt, laid their clothes on them, and set *Him* [Jesus] on them.

This is what sets the Bible apart from other books—you can't beat fulfilled prophecy.

Because there are literally over 150 verses on salvation, I have tried to limit my scope to verses that exclusively apply to God's triune deity. So let's take a quick look at just a few.

In the book of Luke, we are told of a man named Simeon, who was a just man, and it was revealed to him by the Holy Spirit in Luke 2:26 that he would not die until he saw the messiah, Jesus Christ, and the fulfillment of the Holy Spirit's revelation comes a few verses later in Luke 2:30 (ESV), where Simeon, by the Spirit was in the temple, says about Jesus,

> For my eyes have seen your salvation.

What is compelling in these few verses is the direct involvement of the Holy Spirit. God's master plan for the whole world is revealed through the Holy Spirit that the Son of God, the Lord's Christ, is our salvation, and we know this is true because Acts 4:12 (NKJV) says about Jesus,

> Nor is there salvation in any other, for there is no other name under heaven given among men by which we must be saved.

Case closed—and not that the Bible needs to say anything more than once to be true, but if we want to back up the claim of Acts 4:12, we only need to look at 1 Thessalonians 5:9 (KJV) as it reads,

> For God hath not appointed us to wrath, but to obtain salvation by our Lord Jesus Christ,

I know—praise God, right? As Christians, when we accept the Lord as our Savior, we obtain something that we can never lose—salvation! Or as John the Evangelist points out in 1 John 5:13 (NLT),

> I have written this to you who believe in the
> name of the Son of God, so that you may know
> you have eternal life.

As comforting as this verse is to us Christians, there are many Muslims, Jews, and others that put themselves on a set of scales, trying to balance out their bad works (sin) by their good works, hoping that their good works will outweigh their bad. This is not a comforting place to be. Besides, even Paul tells us in his letter to Timothy that salvation is not by works but in Christ as we read 2 Timothy 2:10 (ESV):

> Therefore I endure everything for the sake
> of the elect, that they also may obtain the salva-
> tion that is in Christ Jesus with eternal glory.

As before, the last verse I'd like to share is found in the book of Revelation. Here John puts the Father and Son together again. This is a crescendo of sorts—you have to picture what is taking place. We believers are in heaven and John is witnessing this future event and he sees a multitude of people so large that he says in Revelation 7:9 that it couldn't be numbered, and all were wearing white robes and they were shouting out, proclaiming Revelation 7:10 (ESV):

> Salvation belongs to our God who sits on
> the throne, and to the Lamb!

This coming event is what all Christians long for. We are in heaven, having been redeemed by our Lord, and are praising both God and the Lamb (Jesus). You will notice that both God the Father and Jesus the Lamb are accredited with as having our salvation. There should be no question as to their unique oneness and that it is shared with the Holy Spirit, who, according to John 16:13 (ESV), says,

> When the Spirit of truth comes, he will guide you into all the truth, for he will not speak on his own authority, but whatever he hears He will speak, and he will declare to you the things that are to come. Amen.

CHAPTER 12

PROPHECY

Though I had originally planned on only presenting verses that would prove or extol the trinity of God, I think it is important to slip in this little chapter on prophecy. I think we need to see the confirmation of the prophecies in the Old Testament concerning Jesus the Messiah. If none of the prophecies came true, then it's all a big lie anyway and deserves the least of our attention. However, with amazing accuracy, over three hundred prophecies about Jesus have already come true. Of course, we are all on the edge of eternity, waiting for the rest to be fulfilled.

It has been said—and don't take my word for it, but look these prophecies up yourself—on Empower International, they give the odds of Jesus fulfilling just eight prophecies alone is something like 1in10^17 power (100,000,000,000,000,000). That's a lot of zeros! So, I'd like to share nine prophecies concerning Jesus. I know adding one more prophecy will greatly change the odds, but specifically, I'm not sure how much.

1. First, we know the Messiah was going to be a man as the Old Testament in Isaiah 9:6 (KJV) says,

    For unto us a child is born, unto us a son is given.

And in the New Testament, Mark 6:3 (KJV) says,

Is not this the carpenter, the son of Mary.

2. In the Old Testament in Micah 5:2 (NKJV), it says that the Messiah will be born in Bethlehem:

    But you, Bethlehem Ephrathah, *though* you are little among thousands of Judah, *Yet* out of you shall come forth to Me The One to be Ruler in Israel, Whose goings forth *are* from old, from everlasting.

    This an appropriate verse when speaking of Christ's eternal nature. In the New Testament Gospel of Matthew 2:1 (NKJV)a, we are told about Jesus:

    Now after Jesus was born in Bethlehem of Judea.

    This fulfilled the prophecy found in the book of Micah.

3. I find our third prophecy particularly interesting for the reason that Muslims and Christians alike believe this to be 100 percent true. The Messiah will be born of a virgin! This is announced in the Old Testament book of Isaiah chapter 7, verse 14 (KJV):

    Therefore the Lord himself shall give you a sign; Behold, a virgin shall conceive, and bear a son.

This actually fulfills two prophecies. First, the virgin give birth to a child. Second, the Son being born. In the New Testament's book, Luke 1:27 (KJV) states,

> To a virgin espoused to a man whose name was Joseph, of the house of David; and the virgin's name *was* Mary.

Fascinating because if you study this verse in the Word a little deeper, you know that two prophecies were satisfied again. This occurs as both the house of David and the virgin were both mentioned.

4. About being crucified or hung in a tree, Deuteronomy 21:22–23 (NKJV) says,

> If a man has committed a sin deserving of death, and he is put to death, and you hang him on a tree, his body shall not remain overnight on the tree, but you shall surely bury him that day, so that you do not defile the land which the LORD your God is giving you *as* an inheritance; for he who is hanged *is* accursed of God.

Then again in the New Testament book of Galatians chapter 3 verse 13 (NLT):

> But Christ has rescued us from the curse pronounced by the law. When he was hung on the cross, he took upon himself the curse for our wrongdoing. For it is written in the Scriptures, "Cursed is everyone who is hung on a tree."

5. On the cross, the Messiah was pierced as Zechariah 12:10 (NLT) says,

> They will look on me whom they pierced
> and mourn for him as for an only son.

Moving to the New Testament verse of John 19:34 (NLT), it reveals that while Jesus was hanging on the cross dead,

> One of the soldiers, however, pierced his side with a spear, and immediately blood and water flowed out.

6. Concerning the Passover lamb, Numbers 9:12 (NKJV) in the Old Testament says,

> They shall leave none of it until morning, nor break one of its bones.

And again in John 19:33 (NKJV), it says about the Lamb of God, who was our Sacrifice,

> But when they came to Jesus and saw that He was already dead, they did not break His legs.

7. They will cast lots for the Messiah's clothing. In Psalm 22:18 (KJV) (OT),

> They part my garments among them, and cast lots upon my vesture.

In Mark 15:24 (NKJV), also in the New Testament, it states,

> And when they crucified Him, they divided His garments, casting lots for them to *determine* what every man should take.

8. The Messiah will be rejected as Isaiah 53:3 (KJV) in the Old Testament tells us:

    He is despised and rejected of men.

    In John 1:10–11 (NKJV), we see two more prophecies fulfilled. The verses read,

    He was in the world, and the world was made through Him, and the world did not know Him. He came to His own, and His own did not receive Him.

    This is prophetic Scripture fulfilled.

9. *Okay*, here's the ninth prophecy. This is the test that *all* prophecies rests upon. Without it, no Christianity! In the Old Testament, in the book of Psalms, we read chapter 16, verse 10 (NLT) about Jesus the Messiah:

    For you will not leave my soul among the dead or allow your holy one to rot in the grave.

    This is a discernible and unmistakable reference to Jesus's body *not* decaying after death. In the New Testament, the prophecy from Psalm 16:10 is fulfilled. Matthew 28:5-6 (NKJV) says about Jesus,

    But the angel answered and said to the women, "Do not be afraid, for I know that you seek Jesus who was crucified. He is not here; for He is risen, as He said. Come, see the place where the Lord lay."

A resounding amen for sure. Most certainly, for Christians, the prophetic news of Jesus being raised from the dead is our indisputable hope. Well, there you have it. I actually had a great time looking up prophecies in both testaments. I was surprised about the many prophecies that have been fulfilled and expressed so clearly in New Testament. Did you know that it was prophesied in both the Old and New Testament that the Messiah, Jesus, would be spat on? Or that it was prophesied when the Messiah would enter Jerusalem, placed in a rich man's tomb, or that the Lord would sit at the right hand of God? All in all, I believe there are upwards of 353 prophecies that Jesus has or will fulfill. This is an astounding number indeed. The significant point to all of this is that the Bible and Christianity are the incontrovertible truth. No other holy book makes hundreds of prophecies hundreds of years apart only to have them all come true. I know of no other book that can boast of this. The Qur'an, the Book of Mormon, the Tripitaka in Buddhism, and the Guru Granth Sahib in Sikhism, which is popular in India, do not come close to the historical and prophesied truth found in God's Word, the Bible. It is Christianity alone with its undeniable and accurate history of the Pentateuch, historical books, and prophets in the Old Testament to the restoration of mankind to God the Father through Jesus Christ the Son and the spread of the *Good News* in the New Testament.

Other religions teach of good works to approve yourself as being worthy, whereas in Christianity, we aren't good, but we have a perfect and good Creator, Who alone makes us good by His own sacrifice. The Lord Jesus says that if we believe in Him, He alone will save us from our sin and make us right before God. We do not reach up to Him, but rather, out of His love for us, He reaches down to us. This is the loving heart of God that sent His Son and fills us with His Spirit to complete us.

CHAPTER 13

 formula

JESUS AND DOCTRINE

Though "trinity" and, similarly, "triune" never appear in the Bible, they are clearly taught. If you'll remember, God calls Jesus God. Jesus refers to Himself as God. Jesus's disciples call Him God, and the Bible refers to the Holy Spirit as God. When Jesus's disciple, doubting Thomas, is told of Jesus's resurrection, Thomas proclaimed in John 20:25 (NKJV),

> Unless I see in His hands the print of the nails, and put my finger into the print of the nails, and put my hand into His side, I will not believe.

This is prophetic because Thomas was not there in John 20:24 when Jesus came to visit the disciples after the resurrection. Thomas doubted his fellow disciples when they told him Jesus had appeared to them. With no record of Jesus being told of Thomas's desire to see Jesus's hands, feet, and side, about eight days later, Jesus appeared in a room with all the disciples there including Thomas. The door was shut tight, but Jesus miraculously appeared and said to Thomas in John 20:27 (NLT),

> Put your finger here, and look at my hands.
> Put your hand into the wound in my side. Don't
> be faithless any longer. Believe!

I love this verse because it points once more to Jesus's omniscience. Jesus knew what Thomas had said. In Hebrews 4:13 (NLT), we are told that there is nothing hidden from His sight and

> Nothing in all creation is hidden from God.
> Everything is naked and exposed before his eyes,
> and he is the one to whom we are accountable.

Amen indeed. What comes next after Thomas hears these words from the Lord is nothing short of stunning! Thomas, no doubt, realizing in Whose presence he is in, declares in John 20:28 (NLT),

> My Lord and my God!

Shocking, not only did Jesus not rebuke Thomas for calling Him God; but rather, in John 20:29 (NKJV), He says,

> Thomas, because you have seen Me, you
> have believed. Blessed *are* those who have not
> seen and *yet* have believed.

These are powerful and encouraging words. The disciple Thomas confesses Jesus as God. As I have pointed out earlier in the chapter on Savior, Paul calls Jesus God as well. Convincingly, outside the book of John, the apostle John calls Jesus God again near the end of his first letter in 1 John 5:20 (KJV):

> That we may know him that is true, and we are in him that is true, *even* in His Son Jesus Christ. This is the true God, and eternal life.

We can reference this passage with 1 John 1:1–2 (NKJV) as we read regarding Jesus as the eternal life:

> That which was from the beginning, which we have heard, which we have seen with our eyes, which we have looked upon, and our hands have handled, concerning the Word of life—the life was manifested, and we have seen, and bear witness, and declare to you that eternal life which was with the Father and was manifested to us.

To be sure, Jesus is Eternal life! The author here is talking about Christ from his recollection of the physical Jesus who was with the disciples for three years. They knew Him, ate with Him, touched Him, and were taught by Him. They came to believe that He was God in the flesh. Even the Jews knew that Jesus's claim was making Himself God. When they were about to stone Jesus in John 10:32 (NLT), Jesus said,

> At my Father's direction I have done many good works. For which one are you going to stone me?

And the Jews replied in John 10:33 (NKJV),

> For a good work we do not stone You, but for blasphemy, and because You, being a Man, make Yourself God.

Whoa! They sure got it right. They understood that Jesus was making Himself out to be God. Jesus did this for good reason. Could anyone save us from our sin but God and He alone? Could anyone be worthy of such a great and monumental task? No way! We are saved by no other name but the name of Jesus. We have been cleansed by His blood and are now reconciled to God the Father by faith in Jesus Christ. I think it is a provocative assertion in the New Testament regarding the blood that saves us. The blood is attributed equally to God the Father and God the Son. You should definitely see a triune illustration here. Acts 20:28 (NKJV) says,

> Among which the Holy Spirit has made you overseers, to shepherd the church of God which He purchased with His Own blood.

Plainly, it is by God's redemptive blood that we are saved. In Matthew 26:28 (NLT), as Jesus was eating with His disciples, before He drank from the cup speaking of His sacrifice, He said,

> For this is my blood, which confirms the covenant between God and his people. It is poured out as a sacrifice to forgive the sins of many.

And in 1 John 1:7 (KJV) says,

> But if we walk in the light, as He is in the light, we have fellowship one with another, and the blood of Jesus Christ His Son cleanseth us from all sin.

Lastly, still considering the blood, we can detect the Holy Spirit's connection as we consider 1 John 5:6 (NKJV):

> This is He who came by water and blood— Jesus Christ; not only by water, but by water and

blood. And it is the Spirit who bears witness, because the Spirit is truth.

We can see by this verse that the Spirit participates in the Father/Son triune relationship. There should be no doubt as to the oneness that is shared by the Father, the Son, and that of the Holy Spirit. We see it articulated throughout the Old and New Testament. God is one, and as Scripture shows, He has three unique personages attached to Him—to quote my favorite apologist—"three distinct centers of consciousness."

CONCLUSION

It is really quite simple. Most religions teach that you must perform good works or traditional acts to be considered worthy of their god's less merciful and merited favor. On the other hand, Christianity holds no such "quid pro quo" or "this for that." My going to heaven or your going to heaven is not predicated on anything we can do. It is the 100 percent free gift of God.

Long ago the Jewish people, God's chosen and the ancestral line for Jesus the Messiah, would bring animal sin offerings (the *chatat*) before the LORD. These offerings consisted of an unblemished lamb, bull, or ram for the atonement or pardon of sin. However, they were only considered a temporary covering for sin. Really it was the fulfilling of regulation more than anything else. Under the Mosaic law, the people of God worked to be good by abiding in the law's regulations. Prior to the law, the people of God were saved by believing and having faith in the coming Messiah. Remember Father Abraham? In Genesis 15:6, Abraham had faith, and it was accounted to him as righteousness. According to biblical history and teaching, the coming Messiah Jesus was sinless, perfect, and unblemished. That is why He is called the Lamb of God. In John 1:29 (NKJV), John the Baptist saw Jesus Christ coming near and said,

> Behold! The Lamb of God who takes away
> the sin of the world!

John, by seemingly divine fiat, was pointing out the coming fulfillment of prophecy in the Old Testament. Both Jeremiah 11:19 and Isaiah 53:7 mention the lamb going to the slaughter. When you jump ahead to the New Testament, Jesus is called the lamb. If you read chapter 10 of Hebrews, it denotes there was a sin problem that required a continual blood sacrifice or sin offering. The problem is that the animal sacrifices did not work. Hebrews 10:4 (NLT) says,

> For it is not possible for the blood of bulls
> and goats to take away sins.

So, how does God make a way for us to be cleansed and redeemed? He becomes our Lamb, the propitiation of our sin, our Redeemer and atoning sacrifice. He puts on flesh and becomes a man. He walks a perfect life. Not only does He walk out a perfect life, but He causes the lame to walk, the blind to see, and heals the sick. His perfect life healed our imperfect lives. We have been made clean by the blood of Jesus, God incarnate. As Isaiah 53:4–5 (NKJV) says,

> Surely He has borne our griefs and carried our sorrows; Yet we esteemed Him stricken, Smitten by God, and afflicted. But He *was* wounded for our transgressions [sins], He was bruised for our iniquities; The chastisement for our peace *was* upon Him, and by His stripes we are healed.

Once again, this was Old Testament prophecy being fulfilled by Jesus. He was blameless in all things, and it is only through a blameless Savior that we could ever be found right before a perfect God. As 1 Peter 1:19 (KJV) puts it,

> But with the precious blood of Christ, as of
> a lamb without blemish and without spot.

Only by Jesus's pure blood are we redeemed. The apostle Paul knew this as well. When the Roman jail keeper asked Paul and Silas in Acts 16:30 (KJV),

Sirs, what must I do to be saved?

In Acts 16:31 (KJV), Paul and Silas replied,

Believe on the Lord Jesus Christ, and thou shalt be saved, and thy house.

Sounds simple enough, right? I have a pretty good idea that most of you who haven't made that decision yet are probably thinking, *It can't be that easy? All I need to do is just believe in Jesus as Lord, and I'll be saved?* As I said earlier, it really is just that easy—and thank God that it is that easy. Jesus did all the good work for us and redeemed us on the cross. It is about our faith in Him, not in our good works. No one can boast about good works in His sight. The Bible says of salvation in Ephesians 2:9 (KJV) that it is

Not of works, lest any man should boast.

Even so, here is the good news. Romans 10:9 (NKJV) says,

That if you confess with your mouth the Lord Jesus and believe in your heart that God has raised Him from the dead, you will be saved.

That is the best news ever! It is not about which church you attend, whether you were baptized or not, how many times you've fed the poor, or how much money you give to your favorite charity. It is not about you following some set of laws or regulations perfectly. It is all about what you have done with God's Son, Jesus.

To bring this home, I'd just like to share three more verses. If you are thinking that you want to come to God on your own terms and live life the way you want to, remember these words from the

Lord Jesus Christ. In John 14:6 (NLT), Jesus described Himself in this way:

> I am the way, the truth, and the life. No one
> can come to the Father except through me.

This means your eternal decision and eternal destination are determined by you following Jesus since He is the way and by having fellowship with Jesus since He is the truth and life. Eternity is riding on this. So, if you're thinking, *I'm a good person. There has got to be another way?*

Nope, there is no other way to be saved. But here again, the good part—no matter your ethnicity, race, creed, color, culture, sex, or country—Christianity is all-inclusive! All you have to do is accept Jesus into your heart by faith, repent, or turn from your sin unto God and ask Him for forgiveness. Then thank Him for forgiving you, and He will help you by His Holy Spirit to walk in the way of your new life. If you have already done this, then praise God! You are now a child of God, and you have the everlasting life that He has promised you. We know this because His Word says so. In John 3:16–17 (KJV), Jesus says,

> For God so loved the world that he gave his
> only begotten Son, that whoever believeth in him
> should not perish, but have everlasting life. For
> God sent not His Son into the world to condemn
> the world; but that the world through him might
> be saved.

Amen!

A final thought: As I have said from the beginning, my intention throughout this study was to show Muslims or anyone, for that matter, where we Christians see the Holy Trinity in Scripture. This study was never meant to be all-inclusive and include every reference in God's Word that showed God's nature and His three-personage being. I joyfully invite you to study the truth of the Word of God on your own. You'll be really glad you did.

In Islam, as in other religions, there is a tendency to believe that one must somehow earn God's love. This is an impossible feat. God already loves you, and there is nothing you can do to stop Him from loving you.

There is also nothing you can do to earn His incredible love. For instance, I love my son. My son is a good young man, and I am proud of him. I want him to obey me and do as I ask. I don't want him to ever think he needs to earn my love. He already has my love and knows that I always have his best interests in mind. That is the same as our Father in heaven. When you come to know God, you want to do His will, trusting He has good in store for you. We cannot earn His love because it is freely given. God *is* love.

As Christians, we want to please Him and do His will because we know He loves us so much and because God always has our best in mind.

God is longing and waiting to spend eternity with you in paradise. I urge you right now, if you haven't already, accept Jesus as your Savior and have eternal life.

Eternity begins right now as you have fellowship with Him: God the Father, God the Son, and God the Spirit. Shalom (peace).

ENDORSEMENTS

"The Muslim faith upholds monotheism just like we believe as followers of Jesus. However, Muslims' belief in monotheism is a mixed blessing and a double-edged sword. As a follower of Jesus from a Muslim background, I know Muslims often see the triune God as a stumbling block because they assume that Christians believe in three Gods. As I was exploring and learning about the Christian faith, I struggled with the deity of Jesus. I couldn't believe it in my heart that Jesus is equal with God until the Holy Spirit opened my eyes to see the truth. This book is simple yet powerful. It is an excellent resource for those from a Muslim background who are interested in learning about the Trinity and for anyone who is genuinely seeking to know the truth."

Sahar Saeed—Director of Unveiling Beauty Ministry

"This book is great for helping one understand the triune God we serve. It's an easy study and valuable for new Christians hungry to learn."

Pastor Derek Cowan,
Grace Family Church
Robinson, Texas

About the Author

———————— ⌘ ————————

Mike Barron has a passion to reach Muslims, Mormons, and others unfamiliar with the Bible for the Lord. He has studied Christian apologetics for almost thirty years through attending classes at Calvary Chapel Bible College, home Bible studies, religion-specific studies like EWI (Encountering the World of Islam), and researching on his own.

Mike started out ministry as a Sunday school teacher and has led several men's Bible studies as well as worked on the mission field in Mexico, Belize, and here in the United States. With his degree in criminal justice, he has volunteered with Los Angeles Police Department's "at risk" youth and worked as a volunteer with the county of Riverside, California, for over ten years.

After retiring from the city of Oceanside, California, Mike moved to Texas with his wife and son. He looks forward to seeing how God will use him in the future.

CPSIA information can be obtained
at www.ICGtesting.com
Printed in the USA
BVHW090007171022
649427BV00001B/28

9 798885 408738